Start Early for an Early Start

You and the Young Child

Preschool Services and Parent Education Committee,

Children's Services Division, American Library Association

with the cooperation of

Early Childhood Education Committee,

American Association of School Librarians

FERNE JOHNSON
editor

AMERICAN LIBRARY ASSOCIATION

Chicago

Library of Congress Cataloging in Publication Data

Main entry under title:

Start early for an early start.

    Includes bibliographic references.
    1. Libraries, Children's. 2. Books and reading
for children. I. Johnson, Ferne, 1920-   II. American
Library Association. Preschool Services and Parent
Education Committee. III. American Association of
School Librarians. Early Education Committee.
Z718-1.S74   027.62'5   76-44237
ISBN 0-8389-3185-5

Contents

Foreword

Beginnings are all important. As necessary as the food he eats to build a strong body, the stories, pictures, and song experiences that a small child stores in his mind are resources for coping with and enjoying a complex world.

Teachers at schools for the deaf have long recognized the first six years of life as the peak language-learning period. Now educators everywhere across the country are agreeing with them and carrying the point a step further. Specialists in early childhood education now emphasize that the child's whole attitude toward learning and his success or failure in school is set before he ever enters the institution. In pilot project experiments, trained professionals were sent into the homes to train mothers to play games with their babies, to learn how to exercise babies' muscles and minds to give them every opportunity to retain and develop their innate creative capacities. If we are ever to have a world of peace and equal opportunity for all, we must have men and women able to envision a better way. This pattern can be set in childhood. Einstein was right when he said the best training for a scientist was a sound background and a knowledge of fairy tales.

Libraries are community resource centers. As such, librarians must expand their natural role as leaders in children's programming and reach beyond the children to include the parents. Parents must be led to understand the importance of carefully selecting and using children's materials available to them in their own homes. The fun of sharing and learning together is an extra dividend built into the whole program for parents and children. This dividend will grow as the years pass, and provide the key to eliminating the generation gap that in the past has destroyed and separated families.

Foreword

Annis Duff in her book *Longer Flight* speaks directly to the role of librarians:

> The thing librarians can do for children has a unique value. What they do has standard, direction, stability, growth, and warmth—elements one would always hope to find in the associations and circumstances of a child's living. And there is as well something which, because of their traditional power of sanction, neither the home nor the school is able to effect within itself: a child's absolutely free choice of what use he will make of the advantages offered.... Since the essential function of the Children's Room is to develop the potentialities of books as a rich and strong factor in the child's life, attention is focused on them rather than on the persons involved. This in itself establishes a comfortable sort of situation for a child; he can be utterly himself, and yet not be too conscious of himself.
>
> His relationship with the librarian is in the nature of a partnership in exploration, he setting the compass with his own interests and abilities and responses; she laying the course with skill and knowledge acquired through training and practice. The measure of her success in extending and strengthening a child's powers to explore and assimilate books is determined by her ability to understand what he wants and needs and will enjoy, and by her resourcefulness in providing the right books at the exact right moment of readiness.

Across the United States librarians individually have believed and supported through their work just such a philosophy. They have talked about it at professional meetings large and small, and they have done what they could where they are to experiment and to expand programs.

My own effort has been twofold. In the Westchester Library System we made a film, *The Pleasure Is Mutual,* to train volunteers and professionals in how to conduct effective picture book programs. The film met our need and has been disseminated since in all the fifty states and in five foreign countries. As a second effort, when I was president of Children's Services Division of the American Library Association, I appointed Ferne Johnson to chair the committee on the preschool child. Her sound philosophy, organizational genius, and businesslike procedure produced a true working committee that organized a masterful convention program and went on to write and edit this book. *Start Early for an Early Start* is a practical and inspirational manual for librarians, teachers, community leaders, and most of all for parents, who in the final analysis will open the doors of the world to their children and give them the world we envision.

The separate authors of each section are specialists. As such, each has an individual approach and expertise. No attempt has been made to edit out this individuality, so in each section one learns not only the author's philosophy and technique but also readily sees the writer's style and enthusiasm.

The spontaneity of children and their own great potential keep us all young and eager to meet their needs and desires with the best we have. Ferne Johnson and her committee have made a great contribution.

ANNE R. IZARD

Children's Services Consultant
Westchester Library System
New York State

Preface

The purpose of this book is to provide tested, effective methods, techniques, and resources to help all those interested in the intellectual growth and development of young children. This group includes a very large segment of the population—parents, grandparents, child care personnel, students, teachers, and librarians, to name only a few.

The contributors, all actively engaged in careers directly related to the welfare of young children, have consistently emphasized the why and how of library-related service to preschoolers and to adults responsible for their welfare. The sources of additional information cited in reference lists and bibliographies are selective and meant to be suggestive only.

The programs described are current; their value has been, and in most cases continues to be, documented. Entire projects or selected elements may be adapted with confidence by public and school libraries of any size.

The publication of this book is in response to the many requests for information received by the Preschool Services and Parent Education Committee, Children's Services Division, and the Early Childhood Education Committee, American Association of School Librarians, American Library Association. Application of the ideas and use of the resources suggested herein are sure to help many young children get an "early start."

FERNE JOHNSON

Filmstrips (like literature) can be shared successfully by small children and adults. Photo, taken at Franklin Lakes (N.J.) Free Public Library, courtesy The Record *(Hackensack, N.J.).*

PART 1

The Preschool Child

A child's world is fresh and new and beautiful, full of wonder and excitement.

Rachel Carson,
Sense of Wonder, p. 42

Preschool Profile: Developmental Aspects of Young Children

by Robert L. Doan

That children learn rapidly in the early years has long been questioned, frequently observed, and occasionally rebutted. Until recent years little proof was offered concerning the learning abilities of young children—the three- four- and five-year-olds—who are now often referred to as "preschoolers." This term specifically denotes pre-first grade; therefore, nursery school and kindergarten children are frequently referred to as preschoolers.

Probably the most startling report in recent years relates that by the time a child reaches five years of age, he has developed about half of his intelligence. This seems incredible, but when confronted with such profound statements one should keep a couple of considerations in mind. First, the amount of growth, including brain development, that takes place in a child's first five years is phenomenal. Second, the development of intelligence includes establishing information about persons and things in a child's life, as well as the refinement of mental processes and skills through which learning occurs. These processes include the everyday events in a child's life, such as rolling, sitting, standing, walking, hopping, skipping, running, throwing, catching, communicating with and without language, satisfying needs, learning to learn, and learning to love. This list could go on and on. It would be interesting to compare a list of a preschooler's newly acquired skills and information with that of an adult.

As a child grows and learns, his curiosity and sense of inquiry lead him to investigate thoroughly his nearby surroundings. We've all heard parents say, "That child gets into everything!" The involvement of a young child with his

Robert L. Doan is Associate Professor of Elementary Education, Early Childhood, and Reading, Indiana University at Fort Wayne.

surroundings is much like the ripples set off by a stone thrown into a quiet pond—the circle of ripples becomes wider and wider. As an infant and pre-toddler he explores his room and home thoroughly. By age two or three he has ideas about exploring the "whole world" by spending time in backyard activities. He has developed his walking (and running) skills to a level that enables him to be very mobile. His ability to move about easily decreases the percentage of time and energy needed for mobility and allows more time and energy for investigation, thus increasing the rate of learning and intellectual development.

As the child reaches out for a larger area in which to explore he often meets with a conflict. That conflict is a limitation of space—a barrier—placed by the child's parents. The barrier is not placed to frustrate the child; nor is it placed to limit his curiosity. The simple fact is, safety factors lead most parents to place a limit on how far a child may roam from home. The child's play area may be a backyard or a fenced area or a front sidewalk. No matter what the boundaries, parents rightfully insist that their young children play within range of their supervision. This limited range can and does restrict the child's need to investigate. It is unfortunate, but necessary for safety's sake. This, however, is the time when the nursery school, kindergarten, children's programs in libraries, and child-centered programs of other agencies can become important in the child's life, because this is about the time children really begin playing together.

There are, of course, exceptions, but most children go through several developmental stages of playing (working) with children their own age. The beginning of play is solo play—the child plays alone with a toy or an object of some sort. Therefore, objects—toys, boxes, pots and pans, rattles, balls—have great appeal to him. The next stage of play is parallel play. This means that the child is still playing with a toy or an object or in a sandbox, but alongside (parallel to) another child. He is playing alongside but not with another child because he is inexperienced in interaction with other children. As the child grows through the parallel stage of play, his/her companion gains importance while the importance of the toy or object diminishes. Thus, the beginning of social development in the young child commences.

This is a most appropriate time for a child to attend nursery school, because one of the school's main objectives is to help the child grow socially. Other objectives of most nursery schools include emotional growth, intellectual growth, and physical development. However, striving to attain these objectives is not entirely the responsibility of even the best nursery schools. The home is where childhood education really begins and, hopefully, flourishes. The nursery school can play an effective supportive role in assisting parents by providing special educational opportunities for young children. Other agencies, also, may assist parents in educating the child. Many public libraries

4

provide good—and sometimes extensive—preschool programs. Good day care centers provide much more than mere custodial care. In addition, other community and national agencies are responding to the educational needs of young children and their parents. Ideally, the child's early education begins in the home, is extended through the nursery school, is supplemented by programs of other community agencies, and finally, is further enhanced by a good kindergarten program before he/she enters first grade.

Social Development

Playing and working together is not always easy for children. Such skills do not come naturally; they must be learned. A good nursery school is organized to ease children into group situations. To accomplish this, the nursery school is organized into centers: the housekeeping center, the painting center, an area for blocks, a table for puzzles and crafts, a dress-up corner, a place for train tracks, perhaps a science table and a workbench. While these attractive and tempting work areas are irresistible to young children, their prime purpose is to provide opportunities for two, three, or four children to interact— to have a need to cooperate and communicate. By interacting, children begin to feel comfortable working in small groups.

From time to time the nursery school teacher will draw all the children in the class together. Usually about fifteen or twenty minutes after the children arrive, there will be a whole group activity—an opening song, a finger game, or some form of attendance taking. This short activity brings all the children together for a short period of time. Then teacher and children plan their day and back they go to work centers with two or three other children. Later in the day all the children come together again for story time, for music and rhythms, and for snack time. Gradually the children feel more and more secure in a larger group setting.

Social development means knowing how to get along with other children. This is a very important part of the child's education. If a preschool child has difficulty getting along with others, he will probably have even greater difficulty focusing his attention on whatever learning opportunities become available later. A child who has achieved the skills necessary to get along with others can really concentrate on learning to read when he is in the first grade. The child who has not had the opportunity to achieve these social skills may have difficulty coping with other children and consequently not be able to devote his attention to other tasks.

Parents, teachers, librarians, and child-care personnel who follow the socialization theme believe that the social development of the child is the very core of his growth and development.

The Preschool Child

Emotional Growth

Young children have feelings. Therefore, it is necessary to recognize the child's need to experience his feelings and to try to understand them. However, it is also important for the young child to have knowledgeable supervisors in situations where feelings might get out of control. That is a feature of quality nursery schools, good library programs, and kindergartens. They are set up to allow involvement in planned settings with somewhat structured activities, so children learn to cope with situations and people.

Emotional growth also involves a very important aspect of the personality called self-concept. A person's self-concept means precisely how a person feels about himself. An individual develops a concept of himself on the basis of the way people in his life react to him. If he is made to feel wanted, needed, capable, and enjoyed, he will probably behave as a contributing and enjoyable person. However, if a child perceives himself as unwanted, incapable, and unliked, he will probably behave in a manner that reflects those feelings.

A supportive life inside and outside the home will greatly enhance the chances of a child's developing a positive self-concept.

Intellectual Development

The single most important facet of intellectual growth is probably the development of language skills. It is with language that humans think, communicate, and reason. Therefore, one's reasoning ability, thinking ability, and communicative skills are closely related to the intensity and extensity of language development.

A child develops language by experiencing language as a listener and speaker. It is important, then, that parents and other adults spend some time in realistic conversation with children. It is equally important that adults or young people working with children read appropriate literature to them on a regular basis and provide a variety of opportunities for language experiences, such as dramatization, singing, poetry, and so forth. When children have a rich source from which to develop their language, they are excited and willing to use their skills with others. These experiences further develop the oral language skills basic to other forms of communication.

Another important aspect of intellectual development is the understanding of concepts, understanding who people are, what they do, what they say, and how they act. Children seem to get adult roles sorted out in their minds by observing and then imitating actions. Children play in a housekeeping center, play store, play school, play supermarket, or imitate any of a multitude of adult roles. In this way they try to reenact behavior, use adult conversation, and understand what it is that grown-ups are all about. All these experiences contribute to the intellectual development of young children.

6

Intellectual development cannot be completely understood without thought and insight into intellectual (learning) skills. A simple model of learning is:

Stimulus   Perception   Conceptualization   Response

The stimulus, of course, represents that which is to be learned: a picture, a sound, a process, or whatever. Perception is the stimulus message taken to the brain through the sensory nerves. Conceptualization is the mental absorption of the message. In this step, the message received into the brain is considered, weighed, compared, reviewed, or perhaps even ignored. In the conceptualization step, language is required to think about the message received by the brain. The response step can be in the form of action, a facial expression, a bewildered scratch of the head, a smile, a feeling of response—almost any response appropriate to the manner in which the stimulus was perceived and conceptualized.

It is the second step of this learning model—perception—that is of particular concern. Perceptual skills are learned skills. The home and the preschool have roles in teaching perceptual skills. For the most part visual, auditory, and tactile-kinesthetic (touch-move) skills are the perceptual areas most closely associated with school-like activities. Taste and smell are not considered quite so important in some areas of learning.

Visual perception skills are varied. In addition to determining if a child's eyes are free of disease, it is important to be aware of other areas of visual perception:

1 Figure-ground perception—the ability to see and separate an object from its background
2 Depth perception—the ability to distinguish distance and relative size
3 Directionality—the ability to distinguish, by sight, left-right direction from right-left direction
4 Visual constancy—the ability to retain a constant mental image of an object even when viewing the object from a different angle or in different lighting
5 Ocular pursuit—the ability to smoothly operate the eyes in a coordinated manner when visually tracking a moving object
6 Acuity—clearness of vision, with or without corrective lens
7 Visual motor—the ability to smoothly coordinate movement of a foot or hand in relationship to vision
8 Visual memory—the ability to remember what was observed (There are wide ranging variations.)
9 Visual discrimination—the ability to distinguish one object from another by sight, for example, a circle from an oval, the letter b from d, a square from a rectangle.

The Preschool Child

Auditory skills usually bring to mind only hearing ability. There are, however, at least seven areas of auditory perception that should be considered:

1 Auditory acuity—the ability to hear within normal decibels
2 Auditory processing—sometimes called decoding. This means the ability to accurately perceive the complete auditory message in its proper order
3 Auditory memory—the ability to remember what was heard
4 Auditory discrimination—the ability to distinguish between sounds, for example, sounds that closely resemble one another (m, n), (a, o), (e, i)
5 Auditory screening (for importance)—the ability to focus on some sounds (verbal instructions) and block unnecessary background noise such as passing traffic, a pencil dropping, a person's coughing, and so on
6 Blending—the ability to combine letter sounds into word sounds
7 Sequencing—the ability to perceive and retain auditory stimulation in its proper order.

The tactile-kinesthetic aspect of perception, sometimes called motor skills or muscles movement, relates to how a child moves, controls his body, and blends his motion with what he hears and sees. The smooth operation of body management increases learning because nearly all aspects of learning include the large or small body muscles.

A child's motor skills increase if he has many opportunities to use his body. One of the more common tools currently being used to exercise motor skills is a walking board or balance beam. Using a balance beam requires a coordinated use of vision and muscles. Hopping, skipping, crawling, throwing, and catching are other activities that require coordinated use of vision and motor skills. Since motor skills are closely related to learning, it follows then that physical development is a necessary component in the intellectual development of young children.

Physical Development

Nutritious diet, ample rest, and proper medical care are necessary to the proper physical development of young children. These needs usually should be provided by the home. There are other kinds of physical needs that should be acknowledged at home and outside it. The child has a strong physical need to move. This need is prompted by the growth of large and small muscles in the child's body. Developing muscles need use; they need to be exercised more frequently than mature muscles. Activities for the preschooler should be planned in consideration of the child's need to move and his relatively short attention span. Attempts to retain children in passive activities for long periods are likely to result in conflict.

Creativity

One final aspect of childhood that should be mentioned is creativity. Creativity is difficult to define, but it implies the ability to express feelings in many ways. Too often the term creativity is interpreted to include only artistic skills in graphic arts. A much broader range of expressive skills should be thought of as creative endeavor. The media for expressing creativity should include, but not be limited to, rhythmic expression, painting, clay work, collage making, drama, puppetry, woodworking, dance, and humor. The preschool agencies as well as the home can support a child's creative endeavors by emphasizing and praising process rather than product, and by providing an atmosphere that reaches out to the child and says, "It's okay to try things here. It's okay to make mistakes, too. We learn by being wrong sometimes. Let's try again."

The entire topic of creativity is much too involved to be dealt with effectively here; however, much has been written on the subject. Very worthwhile reading can be found in *The Three-, Four- and Five-Year-Old in a School Setting* by Grace K. Pratt-Butler (Merrill). The many publications of E. Paul Torrance are also recognized as valuable contributions in this field.

Early childhood education is the responsibility of all those who have contact and communication with young children. Primarily, the home has the ultimate responsibility for the total development of the child. However, in a mobile, complex society, the community has a definite influence on early childhood development. The quality of child development, then, is correlated with not only the quality of the home, but also with the quality of community preschools, library programs, child-care agencies, parks and play areas.

References

Davis, David C. *Patterns of Primary Education.* Evanston, Ill.: Harper & Row, Publishers, Inc., 1963.

Chapter 3, "Play," is an enlightening work on the value of play and how children learn through play.

Gordon, Ira J. *The Infant Experience.* Columbus, Ohio: C. E. Merrill Publishing Co., 1975.

This is a comprehensive look into these complicated and important years, including biological and cultural experiences, learning how to learn, and "parenting."

Hymes, James L., Jr. *Before the Child Reads.* Evanston, Ill.: Harper & Row, Publishers, Inc., 1964.

A very short book designed to inform the reader about the concept of "readiness."

———. *Teaching the Child under Six.* 2d ed. Columbus, Ohio: C. E. Merrill Publishing Co., 1974.

This book offers insight into different kinds of programs for young children and the "tools" necessary to teach children.

Leeper, Sarah H., et al. *Good Schools for Young Children: A Guide for Working with Three-, Four-, and Five-Year-Old Children.* 3d ed. New York: Macmillan Publishing Co., 1974.

A guide in child development especially designed for parents, volunteers, aides, preservice teachers, and teachers who have little training in work with young children.

Pratt-Butler, Grace K. *The Three-, Four- and Five-Year-Old in a School Setting.* Columbus, Ohio: C. E. Merrill Publishing Co., 1975.

Chapter 6, "Creative Expression," covers the feelings and expressiveness of children.

Talbot, Tony, ed. *The World of the Child.* Garden City, N.Y.: Doubleday & Company, 1967.

This book is a collection of famous essays on children, covering such topics as "The Nature of Childhood," "Individual Growth," "A Child Reacts...," and "The Training and Education of a Child." The contributing writers include Phillipe Aries, Carl Jung, Jean Piaget, Jean-Jacques Rousseau, and John Dewey.

Bibliography

Hildebrand, Verna. *Guiding Young Children.* New York: Macmillan Publishing Co., 1975.

Leeper, Sarah H., et al. *Good Schools for Young Children.* 3d ed. New York: Macmillan Publishing Co., 1974.

Machado, J. M. *Early Childhood Experiences in Language Arts.* Albany, N.Y.: Delmar Publishers, 1975.

Mayesky, Mary. *Creative Activities for Young Children.* Albany, N.Y.: Delmar Publishers, 1975.

Smart, M. S., and R. C. Smart. *Preschool Children.* New York: Macmillan Publishing Co., 1975.

Winick, M. P. *Before the 3R's.* New York: David McKay, 1973.

PART 2

Parent/Child Interaction

*Sensory and intellectual stimulation,
plus freedom to explore and research his world,
add up to the early development
of his intellectual capacity.*

Fitzhugh Dodson,
How to Parent, p. 72

Learning Experience with Infants

by Harriet R. Fuller and Bonnie J. Stuelpe

Most techniques for using books and music with young children have been aimed at the three-, four- and five-year-old, while little or no emphasis has been placed upon the importance of learning experiences for infants (babies and one- and two-year-old children). The reason, of course, is that, to the untrained observer, an infant shows little reaction to people or things and thus is apparently capable of little learning.

Piaget's view offers a strong contrast to this conception of the newborn as a predominantly helpless and inactive creature, for he characterized the newborn as active and as an initiator of behavior. The infant quickly learns to distinguish among various features of the immediate environment and to modify his behavior in accordance with their demands. In fact, his activity reveals the "origins of intelligence."[1]

Based upon relatively recent research by Piaget and other noted psychologists, parents and other adults involved with children must acknowledge the importance of providing learning experiences for the infant in order to foster his intellectual development. As Benjamin Bloom concludes in *Stability and*

---

1. Herbert Ginsburg and Sylvia Opper, *Piaget's Theory of Intellectual Development: An Introduction* (© 1969), p. 27. Reprinted by permission of Prentice-Hall, Inc., Englewood Cliffs, New Jersey.

Harriet R. Fuller is Branch Librarian, Memphis–Shelby County Public Library and Information Center, Memphis, Tennessee. Bonnie J. Stuelpe is Supervisor, Elementary Instructional Media, Fort Wayne Community Schools, Fort Wayne, Indiana.

Parent/Child Interaction

Change in Human Characteristics, a study based upon 1,000 different studies of infant growth, "These results [of longitudinal intelligence studies] also reveal the changing rate at which intelligence develops, since as much of the development takes place in the first 4 years of life as in the next 13 years."[2] Thus, during these very early years parents greatly influence the child's future intelligence and his learning potential.

If parents and the other adults who minister to the infant's needs provide him with an abundance of learning experiences, they not only contribute to his intellectual development, but they also help to create a positive attitude toward learning. Knowledge gained from these early experiences gives the child the self-confidence needed to help him perceive kindergarten and elementary school as easy and fun. As Aidan Chambers has said, "Readers are made, not born. No one comes into the world already disposed for or against words in print."[3] Thus, parents and those other adults close to the child must help him to form the basic attitudes important to literacy and learning.

Learning experiences for the very young child also contribute to his emotional development. When an infant is held and read to, or a song is sung to him, a highly intimate and personal relationship develops between him and the adult. He knows that he is loved and watched over; he feels secure. Stories, poetry, and songs provide opportune situations for involving the adult in the toddler's "world of activity." This involvement verifies the infant's activities and gives him the confidence necessary for coping with his emotions and actions; it provides him with the self-security essential for continued exploration. As he grows older, this sense of security will be reflected in his relationship to others and in his ability to deal with an ever-expanding environment.

When should an adult begin to provide learning experiences for the infant? Some experts recommend beginning as soon as the infant is brought home from the hospital. The human baby has the ability to understand and distinguish various sound patterns almost from the moment of birth. He begins to develop comprehension skills early in infancy because he is constantly applying meanings to the sounds he hears. Therefore, during the first six months of an infant's life, while his visual abilities are developing, learning experiences should be centered around sound and spoken language rather than around printed or pictorial material.

Learning activities for the young baby are instinctively performed by many adults. Who has not trotted a baby on his knee to "Ride a Cock Horse" or played "Patty Cake"? Who has not used "Rock-a-Bye Baby" to soothe a child

---

2. Benjamin S. Bloom, *Stability and Change in Human Characteristics* (New York: John Wiley & Sons, 1964), p. 88. Reprinted by permission of John Wiley & Sons, Inc.

3. Aidan Chambers, *Introducing Books to Children* (London: Heineman Educational Books, 1973; copies of the publisher's edition are available in the United States from the Horn Book, Inc., Boston), p. 16. Reprinted by permission of the publishers.

to sleep or greeted him in the morning with "Good Morning to You"? These simple nursery rhymes and songs allow him to hear repetitive phrases and to obtain a feeling for the rhythm and music of spoken language.

Through listening to adult conversation and speech and through hearing nursery rhymes, songs, and lullabies during these early months, the child learns to listen with discrimination to words and sounds. He begins to pay attention to intensity, pitch, tone, quality, and duration of words. This ability to listen with discrimination is one of the most important skills in the development of verbal facility, a vital competency in the making of a reader.

Near the end of his first year, when eyesight is more developed and verbalization begins to take place, the infant should be exposed to large, simple pictures. In this way he can begin developing the important skill of interpreting pictures and coupling words with objects in both listening and speaking activities.

One way to provide pictures is to cut them out of old magazines and attach them to a wall or bulletin board near the infant's crib. Adults should select objects familiar to the infant and of interest to him. Animals, people, and simple action pictures are good choices. The parent or other adult should give the name of the object in the picture so the child may repeat it after him. The objective of this activity is to get the child to verbalize about what he sees in the pictures. Constant practice and repetition are important.

Picture books of single objects can also be examined daily, with the adult pointing to and giving names of objects viewed. These sessions should be very short, scheduled when the child needs a calming activity or is ready for a daily quiet time. The physical contact between adult and infant during such periods adds an important dimension to the child's emotional development.

While the child is developing a proficiency in oral interpretation of pictures, he is also forming a bank of meaningful words to draw upon to understand meanings of other words and phrases in future reading and listening activities. These early experiences with oral language are important to the child's intellectual development, because his progress in identification of objects and events will help him clarify his own world.

During this period of time, musical stimulation should continue. Baby rattles, bells, measuring spoons, wooden blocks—items which a baby can safely manipulate in order to produce sounds—will provide aural stimulation, thus improving both his listening skills and his physical dexterity. The use of nursery rhymes and songs should continue. "Rub-a-Dub-Dub" can enhance bathtime pleasure. Identifying natural phenomena can be encouraged with "I See the Moon," "Rain, Rain, Go Away," and so on. The sharing of such activities provides pleasure for both the child and the adult and additional learning experiences for the child.

Storytelling and reading aloud from simple picture books should begin

Parent/Child Interaction

during the infant's second year. Book experiences are important to the intellectual development of the infant since they contribute to an environment that is active and stimulating. "The greater the variety of pleasurable social and intellectual stimulation in infancy, the greater the child's capacity for development later."[4]

Parents and other concerned adults should plan a regular time for reading aloud with the infant. Just before naptime or bedtime are good choices. It is not necessary for the experience to last for many minutes since a child of this age has a limited attention span. If he becomes restless or bored, it is better to stop than to make him continue. It is his pleasure in the learning situation that is important.

There is a wide variety of picture books from which to choose. Those which give names to objects that the child sees, hears, touches, and holds in his everyday life are good starters. A picture dictionary such as *Colors* or a large alphabet book such as *Brian Wildsmith's ABC* provides an opportunity for the child to practice verbalizing about what he sees. *Mr. Brown Can Moo, Can You?* provides the opportunity for sound reproduction. Parts of the body and their functions can be introduced by *The Eye Book, The Nose Book,* and *The Foot Book.* Picture books that help the child to develop a good number sense can also be shared in the reading-aloud period. *Brian Wildsmith's 1, 2, 3* and the *Sesame Street Book of Numbers* are good examples.

Later in the second year, books containing more printed text can be used. Rhyming texts such as *Old Hat, New Hat* and *Dr. Seuss's ABC* allow the child to hear the rhythm and musical quality of language. Personal relationships can be reinforced through the use of simple family stories like *Whose Mouse Are You?* and *Are You My Mother?* These experiences also prepare the young child for learning to read by helping with vocabulary development, comprehension skills, and visual discrimination.

It is during this second year that the toddler should learn to handle books by himself. Cloth books of either commercial or home origin are recommended starter books to minimize destruction. Once the child is able to turn pages successfully, old magazines and merchandise catalogs make good learning tools; they are bright, colorful, and provide an opportunity to practice visual discrimination and verbalization. Later, inexpensive Golden Books or Tell A Tale Books can be purchased.

Infants learn their attitudes toward books and reading from the people around them. "Quite obviously, as most children spend their infant years, which is the important period in socialization, aware of very few people, usually members of their family, it is from them, parents, brothers and sisters,

---

4. Lillian and Richard Peairs, *What Every Child Needs* (New York: Harper & Row, Publishers, Inc., 1974), p. 298.

Learning Experience with Infants

attendant relatives and friends, that they learn the primary adaptive lessons. Naturally, how these people regard books, how much they read and talk about what they read, how many books they buy and borrow, keep about them and value, will be part of the way of life absorbed by their children almost as if by osmosis."[5] Newspapers and magazines should be shared with the young child. In this way, the infant will absorb a way of life which includes books and reading experiences.

Music activities should also be increased during the child's second year. Simple songs such as "Old MacDonald" and "Farmer in the Dell" can be shared with the infant; after much repetition he will begin to participate. Once he has gained stability in walking, musical games such as "Ring around the Rosey," "London Bridge," and a musical "Follow the Leader" will improve physical coordination and provide exposure to various rhythms. Basic rhythm instruments such as coffee can drums, or pans and spoons, can be given to the child. He should be encouraged to respond to music provided for him by the adult. At this age he will also begin to enjoy listening to records, particularly those which are broken into many short segments. *Walt Disney's Mother Goose* or the Sesame Street albums are good examples.

During the child's third year all the activities begun in his second year can be increased and expanded. Since his attention span is longer, the use of single-object picture books can be decreased and more complex family or animal stories can be introduced. The *Tale of Peter Rabbit* and *Whistle for Willie* are good examples. Wordless picture books also provide excellent learning experiences for the young child. *Making Friends* and *Frog, Where Are You?* will allow the child to practice visual discrimination and gain skill in comprehending what he sees; and since he is now able to communicate in short sentences, the toddler should be encouraged to share his reactions. The use of poetry should also be increased during this time. Poetry adapts particularly well to times that are special to the child, such as birthdays and holidays.

Since book experiences are provided in order to help the child develop verbal facility, these activities should be characterized by much sharing of conversation. Questions should be asked and answered. The child should be made to feel that his comments are valid and important. Adult responses should be in the vocabulary of the adult interspersed with definitions of new or difficult words. Pronunciation should be precise, and word endings must not be slurred or dropped.

Music activities should also be increased during the third year. Many three-year-old children can operate simple record players. Peter Pan Records and Walt Disney Productions produce inexpensive book/record sets that the child can enjoy by himself or share with an adult. Dancing with a large doll or a

---

5. Chambers, *Introducing Books to Children,* p. 16. Reprinted by permission of the publishers.

broom to such classics as "March of the Toreadors" or "The Blue Danube Waltz" is not only fun but allows the child to improve physical coordination and respond to feelings evoked by the music. Popular rock music provides opportunities for practice with rhythm instruments. Children at this age will also begin to sing. Ella Jenkins, the noted collector of ethnic music, has developed a "call and response" method for uniting children and music. Young children respond enthusiastically to any of her records.

It cannot be overemphasized that learning experiences are vital to the total development of the infant and greatly affect his future potential. The school-age child who has not had access to the types of learning experiences discussed here has passed through his most fertile period of growth without the stimulation essential to intellectual and personal growth. Parents, teachers, librarians—all concerned adults—should strive to provide the infant with stimulating and varied learning experiences that will help him fulfill his potential in all areas of development: physical, social, emotional, and intellectual.

References

Ames, Louise Bates. *Child Care and Development.* Philadelphia: J. B. Lippincott & Co., 1970.

Bloom, Benjamin S. *Stability and Change in Human Characteristics.* New York: John Wiley & Sons, 1964.

Braga, J. D. *Child Development and Early Childhood Education.* Chicago: Model Cities—Chicago Committee on Urban Opportunity, 1973.

Brearley, Molly, ed. *The Teaching of Young Children: Some Applications of Piaget's Learning Theory.* New York: Schocken Books, 1969.

Chambers, Aidan. "The Making of a Literary Reader." *Hornbook* 51:301–10 (June 1975).

Doman, Glenn. *How to Teach Your Baby to Read–The Gentle Revolution.* New York: Random House, 1964.

Ginsburg, Herbert, and Opper, Sylvia. *Piaget's Theory of Intellectual Development: An Introduction.* Englewood Cliffs, N.J.: Prentice-Hall, 1969.

Hughes, Felicity. *Reading and Writing before School.* New York: St. Martin's Press, 1971.

Larrick, Nancy. *A Parent's Guide to Children's Reading.* 4th rev. ed. Garden City, N.Y.: Doubleday & Company, 1975.

Painter, Genevieve. *Teach Your Baby.* New York: Simon & Schuster, 1971.

Peairs, Lillian, and Richard H. Peairs. *What Every Child Needs.* New York: Harper & Row, Publishers, Inc., 1974.

Tinker, Miles A. *Preparing Your Child for Reading.* New York: Holt, Rinehart & Winston, 1971.

Woodward, O. M. *Earliest Years: Growth and Development of Children under Five.* Elmsford, N.Y.: Pergamon Press, 1966.

Titles for Infants and Those Who Work with Infants

A B C BOOKS

Matthiesen, Thomas. *ABC.* Bronx, N.Y.: Platt & Munk Publishers, 1966.

Oxenbury, Helen. *Helen Oxenbury's ABC of Things.* New York: Franklin Watts, 1971.

Piatti, Celestino. *Celestino Piatti's Animal ABC.* New York: Atheneum Publishers, 1966.

Seuss, Dr. *Dr. Seuss's ABC.* New York: Random House, 1963.

Wildsmith, Brian. *Brian Wildsmith's ABC.* New York: Franklin Watts, 1962.

COUNTING BOOKS

Carle, Eric. *Very Hungry Caterpillar.* Cleveland: William Collins & World Publishing Co., 1972.

Children's Television Workshop, eds. *Sesame Street Book of Numbers.* New York: W. W. Norton & Co., 1971.

Keats, Ezra Jack. *Over in the Meadow.* New York: Scholastic Book Services, 1972.

Sugita, Yataka. *Good Night, 1, 2, 3.* New York: Scroll Press, 1971.

Wildsmith, Brian. *Brian Wildsmith's 1, 2, 3.* New York: Franklin Watts, 1965.

MOTHER GOOSE BOOKS

Anglund, Joan W. *In a Pumpkin Shell: A Mother Goose ABC.* New York: Harcourt Brace Jovanovich, 1960.

Briggs, Raymond, comp. *The Mother Goose Treasury.* New York: Coward, McCann & Geoghegan, 1966.

De Angeli, Marguerite. *Pocket Full of Posies.* New York: Doubleday & Co., 1961.

Real Mother Goose. Chicago: Rand McNally & Co., 1944.

Wildsmith, Brian. *Brian Wildsmith's Mother Goose.* New York: Franklin Watts, 1964.

NURSERY RHYME BOOKS

Bertail, Inez, comp. *Complete Nursery Song Book.* New York: Lothrop, Lee & Shepard Co., 1954.

Lines, Kathleen, comp. *Lavender's Blue.* New York: Franklin Watts, 1969.

Montgomery, Norah. *This Little Pig Went to Market.* New York: Franklin Watts, 1966.

Opie, Iona, and Peter Opie. *Family Book of Nursery Rhymes.* New York: Oxford University Press, 1964.

Rossetti, Christina. *Sing Song: A Nursery Rhyme Book.* New York: Macmillan Publishing Co., 1968.

Parent/Child Interaction

SONGS AND FINGERPLAYS

Glazer, Tom. *Eye Winker, Tom Tinker, Chin Chopper: A Collection of Musical Finger Plays.* New York: Doubleday & Co., 1972.

Kapp, Paul. *A Cat Came Fiddling and Other Rhymes of Childhood.* New York: Harcourt Brace Jovanovich, 1956.

Mitchell, Donald, sel. *Every Child's Book of Nursery Songs.* Santa Cruz, Cal.: Bonanza Press, 1968.

Poston, Elizabeth. *Baby's Song Book.* New York: Thomas Y. Crowell, 1971.

Winn, Marie, and Allan Miller. *Fireside Book of Children's Songs.* New York: Simon & Schuster, 1966.

POETRY

Frank, Josette, ed. *Poems to Read to the Very Young.* New York: Random House, 1961.

Opie, Peter, and Iona Opie, eds. *Oxford Book of Children's Verse.* New York: Oxford University Press, 1973.

Stevenson, Burton Egbert, ed. *Home Book of Verse for Young Folks.* rev. ed. New York: Holt, Rinehart & Winston, 1930.

ANIMAL BOOKS

Munari, Bruno. *Bruno Munari's Zoo.* Cleveland: William Collins & World Publishing Co., 1961.

Provensen, Alice, and Mark Provensen. *Our Animal Friends at Maple Hill Farm.* New York: Random House, 1974.

Rojankovsky, Feodor. *Animals in the Zoo.* New York: Alfred A. Knopf, 1962.

———. *Animals on the Farm.* New York: Alfred A. Knopf, 1967.

Wildsmith, Brian. *Brian Wildsmith's Wild Animals.* New York: Franklin Watts, 1967.

FAMILY STORIES

Eastman, Philip D. *Are You My Mother?* New York: Random House, 1960.

Hoff, Syd. *The Horse in Harry's Room.* New York: Harper & Row, Publishers, Inc., 1970.

Keats, Ezra Jack. *Whistle for Willie.* New York: Viking Press, 1964.

Kraus, Robert. *Whose Mouse Are You?* New York: Macmillan Publishing Co., 1970.

Potter, Beatrix. *Tale of Peter Rabbit.* New York: Frederick Warne & Co., 1902.

WORDLESS PICTURE BOOKS

Carroll, Ruth. *What Whiskers Did.* New York: Henry Z. Walck, 1965.

Hartelius, Margaret A. *The Chicken's Child.* New York: Doubleday & Co., 1975.
Keats, Ezra Jack. *Pssst, Doggie.* New York: Franklin Watts, 1973.
Mayer, Mercer. *Frog, Where Are You?* New York: Dial Press, 1969.
Schick, Eleanor. *Making Friends.* New York: Macmillan Publishing Co., 1969.

PHONOGRAPH RECORDS
Columbia Records. Sesame Street Albums. 45 or $33\frac{1}{3}$ rpm.
Disney Productions. Book/Record Sets. 45 or $33\frac{1}{3}$ rpm.
Peter Pan Productions. Book/Record Sets. 45 or $33\frac{1}{3}$ rpm.
Scholastic Records. Early Childhood Records by Ella Jenkins. $33\frac{1}{3}$ rpm.

PAMPHLETS FOR PARENTS
Children's Book Committee, Child Study Association of America. *Reading with Your Child through Age Five.* rev. ed. New York: Child Study Press, 1972.
Children's Services Division of the American Library Association, Committee on Library Service to the Disadvantaged Child. *Reading Aloud to Children.* Chicago: American Library Association, 1967.
Choosing a Child's Book. New York: Children's Book Council, 1970.
Parents Can Teach Pre-Reading Skills at Home. Prepared by the National Reading Center. Washington, D.C.: U.S. Govt. Printing Office, 1971. Stock No. 1780-0921.
Reading Begins at Home. Chicago: American Library Association, 1974.

Toys That Teach

by Nancy Young Orr

I n Montgomery County, Maryland, the cooperation and shared expertise of a number of different county agencies and organizations have brought into being a pilot library project called "Toys That Teach." The children's services division of the Department of Public Libraries has for many years offered active support to a wide range of early childhood programs in the county, but had not considered toy lending until the local chapter of the Association for Childhood Education broached the idea in the spring of 1973. This organization offered the public library a grant of $500 to establish a pilot toy library in the county. Though the concept of toy lending was new and foreign to the children's services staff, this gift was accepted as an opportunity to learn with some expert help. Along with the gift came the guidance of an advisory committee that included the Parent Education Specialist of the Montgomery County Public Schools.

At an initial meeting many policy decisions were made. In a county system of seventeen branches and two bookmobiles, serving 580,000 people, $500 clearly would not buy enough toys for general circulation. In addition, the library administration did not feel that toy lending per se was a justifiable extension of service; a logical focus was needed. The library staff wanted to design a pilot project that would serve a real child need in the county, and would, in addition, make some impact on the larger community that could not be served directly.

The decision was made to limit toy borrowing to Family Day Care homes licensed by the Department of Social Services, and to the parent users of the homes, and to link toy use to a series of training meetings. Throughout the

Nancy Young Orr is Assistant Coordinator of Children's Services, Montgomery County Department of Public Libraries, Rockville, Maryland.

county the library had already established regular visits, story hours, and book lending to children in day care centers; toy lending seemed a way of reaching out to children being cared for in homes. It was decided that the target age would be from eighteen months through three-and-a-half years–the ages of children more often cared for in homes. Through the toy project an effort would be made to strengthen the role of Family Day Care mothers, help them realize the importance of their role as teachers, and encourage them to interact with children and with each other.

Language development, however, was selected as the major goal of the project. Many research studies demonstrate the enormous amount of language growth that takes place in the first three years of life. Play experiences with adult interaction can be valuable in stimulating verbal competence in young children, and the Family Day Care mother is in a position to be a powerful influence on early development. Also this goal seemed to provide a natural link with the use of the library for books and other services.

Five basic toys were selected in duplicates of ten to be used in a series of five training meetings. Ten additional, more advanced toys were chosen to be freely borrowed by Family Day Care mothers after completion of the training course. Later about twenty more toys, including a greater proportion of puzzles, were added. The staff members were glad they had not spent all the budget at once and could go out and choose toys to meet identified needs and interests.

Each toy was selected for its built-in capacity for developing concepts such as size, shape, labeling, color matching, language expansion, or spatial relationships. Individual brochures were designed to go with each of the five basic toys. Each brochure pointed out some specific learning dimensions of the toy and in addition offered a few general comments about play, learning, and adult-child interaction, always adding, "Enjoy yourself. Have a good time playing with your child." A book title was selected to coordinate with each toy. (Books were purchased with library funds.) The toys and companion books selected for use in the five training sessions were.

Col-O-Rol Wagon (Playskool 303)–Hoban, *Push-Pull, Empty-Full*
Wooden Shape Puzzle (Connor Toy 6055)–Gay, *Look!*
Klickety-Klack Express (Kusan 25)–Zaffo, *Big Book of Real Trains* (This train was selected because of sequential linking but has not proved sturdy enough for heavy use.)
Building Cups (Playskool 1039) or Barrels (Child Guidance)–Gretz, *Teddy Bears 1 to 10*
School Bus (Fisher-Price 192)–One of three books: Krauss, *Bundle Book;* Keats, *Whistle for Willie;* Keats, *Peter's Chair*

While the "Toys That Teach" project has been tailored to local situations and needs, useful program models were the Parent/Child Toy-Lending Library of the Far West Laboratory for Educational Research and Development, and the Verbal Interaction Project of the Family Service Association of Nassau County, New York.

Volunteers from RSVP (Retired Senior Volunteer Program) made drawstring bags to hold each toy and book set. Bright squares in primary colors were appliqued on each sailcloth bag to identify the basic toys in sequence, from one through five. The pleasure of the two women who cheerfully arrived in the library offices each week to sew made this project more meaningful for all involved. Very recently a group of RSVP men created ten beautiful sorting boxes in a home workshop and contributed them to the program. Being able to take advantage of the help offered by this volunteer group gave the project an even broader community base.

The Silver Spring (branch) Library was selected as the location of the pilot project. This branch serves a densely populated, urban area of the county and is geographically central to a great many Family Day Care homes. It also has a children's services staff totally committed to and experienced in service to young children. Fortunately, the staff had available time to devote to this new project. Furthermore, this branch has basement stack space available to house the toys—an important consideration.

The Parent Education Specialist held a training session for the library staff. At this time she introduced the role-playing technique which would be used and explained each basic toy, pointing out the possibilities for interaction and the learning potential it offered. All interested staff members were welcome at this session. The Parent Education Specialist also conducted the first series of training classes for parents. Library staff were scheduled as observers at these classes, one at a time so as not to intimidate the group. The comments and suggestions of staff observers proved constructive and helpful.

With this help in getting started, the library took over the entire project. The head of the Silver Spring children's room conducted the subsequent workshops with Family Day Care mothers, with helpful consultation, and advice as questions arose, from the Parent Education Specialist. Because of her special interest, a member of the staff of the Noyes Library, a branch for children, assumed the role of Project Coordinator, giving additional support and working especially to extend the impact beyond the Family Day Care homes that are served directly.

The Family Day Care Unit in the Department of Social Services has distributed information flyers about the project, publicized it through a newsletter, and registered Family Day Care mothers as participants. A maximum of eight parents may be registered for each series of "Toys That Teach" workshop sessions. Meetings last for an hour and are held weekly, at first for five weeks but now for four, with two toys (instead of one) presented at the third or fourth session. Family Day Care parents who complete the workshop are issued a special card entitling them to borrow (for a two-week loan period) from a selection of other toys.

This rather bare-bones description of the structure of the project cannot convey the human dimension of each workshop session. A new toy is introduced as it might be presented to a child, with the leader role-playing the parent and the participants encouraged to respond as if they were children. The approach is to allow the child to freely explore and to suggest positive actions, rather than using "don't" or negative responses. The importance of respecting each child's style of learning and allowing him to make discoveries for himself is emphasized. At the same time, interaction with the child is encouraged as is language input with use of exact words and phrases for labeling, classifying, and describing actions. The toys are used as a focus for adult-child interaction, but neither the specific use of the toy nor purely cognitive learning is considered as important as the development of the whole child.

At every session an example of a homemade toy or use of household materials for child learning and play is also presented. The companion book is also introduced by the leader, with a resulting sense of appreciative discovery often expressed. One treasured remark was, "I never knew the public library had such great books for two-year-olds." After the first class, mothers discuss among themselves experiences they have had with the borrowed toy and with their children. Ideas for using the toys for fun and for language development are enthusiastically shared as the group feels more at ease and becomes more familiar with the techniques and concepts.

At the end of the final workshop session, parents are taken into the children's room of the library to see a temptingly arranged display of materials, including many of the toys available for free borrowing.

Library staff members have learned a great deal from following through on this pilot project. Some of the lessons in group dynamics possibly have to be learned firsthand—how to handle competing personalities in a group, and the need to structure role-playing to keep discussion pertinent. Experience has also shown that it is inadvisable to schedule workshop sessions just before Christmas. The total number of parents and children reached is still small; however, support for continuing the project has come from both workshop participants and day care supervisory staff.

A recent publication on child care services states:

> The bulk of child care available and used by working mothers in this country is in a family day care home.
> ...Coordinating groups must be made aware of the desperate need to bring licensed home operators into communication with each other, ...help them upgrade the services they could offer. When this begins,

nonlicensed operators can become aware of the advantages of becoming licensed and affiliated with such a group.

...More and more we are realizing that the stigma of custodial care often attached to day care homes can be eliminated and day care mothers, often warm, loving, caring people, are more than willing to learn how to be better providers of child care.[1]

Montgomery County's experience certainly bears out this statement. The Family Day Care supervisor in the Department of Social Services is enthusiastic about the "Toys That Teach" project and now considers it an important component of their program—enough so that they have included funds for project expansion in their next budget request. The majority of the Family Day Care mothers recruited for an optional child-development class which the agency offered had been "Toys That Teach" participants, an indication of the motivation and the awareness of early learning potential that the program has generated. Day care staff state that the program has opened communications, and that day care mothers who have participated are reading to children, are aware of and interested in teaching concepts, and are not just plopping the children in front of the television.

In spite of these glowing comments, recruitment has not been as easy as had been expected. A woman who has cared for up to four lively preschoolers all day long, often in addition to a child of her own, is low on energy at the end of the day and needs tremendous motivation to come to an evening class. "Why should I go to the library to learn about toys?" is often the initial reaction. Word-of-mouth is the best advertising, and past participants are the most effective spokeswomen for the program. An exhibit and presentation of toys at a Sunday afternoon reception for all Family Day Care mothers in the county generated much interest and a number of new registrations. Library staff members are going to try a second pattern of scheduling—morning meetings, with two small groups meeting on different days, alternating babysitting for one another. They are also considering planning a group of classes for parents of hearing-impaired preschoolers and opening toy borrowing to them.

Plans are being made to expand the "Toys That Teach" project to a second location in the county, a new branch building which will open in a few months and is central to a second area with a large concentration of Family Day Care homes. Again, able and interested staffers are available and willing to learn new skills and undertake this new service.

No funds are available from the library budget to purchase more toys, and the budget request from Social Services is not at all assured in this lean year.

---

1. Patricia Ratliff, *Organizing to Coordinate Child Care Services* (Washington, D.C.: Day Care and Child Development Council of America, 1973), pp. 47, 48, 51.

However, the cost of toys is not a major deterrent. The library staff will be working with the very willing and capable RSVP volunteers who will duplicate some toys in home workshops; it is hoped too that gifts can be found to fund toy purchase.

A second goal of the pilot project has also been reached—that of sharing its concepts with the community at large. Chief among these concepts is the important principle of using toys as a medium for parent/child interaction. In designing the project the library administration was concerned about positive public relations and felt that this investment of staff energy for a relatively small user group should have as much spin-off as possible for all parents of young children.

This concern has been alleviated in a number of ways. The five brochures that accompany the five basic toys are available to any parent in all county libraries. A demonstration set of toys has been scheduled for display in many of the branches. The Project Coordinator has given "Toys That Teach" talks to parents of children during library preschool story hours, often with a younger sibling as a delighted toy-demonstrator. Also she has conducted a workshop session, "Books to Grow On: Toys That Teach," for the annual Maryland Conference of Parent Participation Nursery Schools. The toy brochures and the project concepts have become a natural part of the library's presentation of books and library materials at the many talks given to nursery school mothers and other groups interested in early childhood.

Furthermore, there is no doubt that this project has had a tremendous influence on our total staff of children's librarians, helping them to recognize and meet learning needs of very young children. The regular programs have been enriched by the occasional use of a toy along with books. (Toys in the second set may be reserved by any branch for use in a program.) More use is being made of realia in story hour programs and in visits with day care centers and nursery schools.

One example of a creative linking of media is the use of the film *Changes, Changes* along with the book of the same title by Pat Hutchins and a bag of brightly colored blocks. The librarian introduces the film by showing blocks, talking about changes in things a child can build, and then encouraging the children to talk about each page of the book and anticipate what the little wooden couple will build next. Showing the film after this introduction always seems to unleash imaginations, and playing with the blocks handed out becomes a joyful experience for small groups of three- and four-year-olds as well as for parents and teachers.

Montgomery County's experience with toys has been one impetus for the development of multi-media "discovery centers" in the Noyes Children's Library, a concept which hopefully will be extended throughout the system. As library staff members look back on what has happened with "Toys That

Teach," they recognize the truth of Roethke's "I learn by going where I have to go."[2] By working with many other agencies in the county, staff members have turned into reality the maxim adopted for all of the toy brochures, "Children LEARN while they PLAY. Children learn MORE when PARENTS play WITH them."

Bibliography

Changes, Changes (film). Color. 6 min. 16mm. Weston, Conn.: Weston Woods, 1972.

Far West Laboratory for Educational Research and Development. *A Guide to Securing and Installing the Parent/Child Toy-Lending Library.* Washington, D.C.: U.S. Govt. Printing Office, 1972.

Gordon, Ira, et al. *Child Learning through Child Play: Learning Activities for Two- and Three-Year Olds.* New York: St. Martin's Press, 1972.

Marzallo, Jean, and Lloyd, Janice. *Learning through Play.* New York: Harper & Row, Publishers, Inc., 1972.

Ratliff, Patricia. *Organizing to Coordinate Child Care Services.* With an appendix, "The Greater Minneapolis Day Care Association: Early History," by Pauline Berryman. Washington, D.C.: Day Care and Child Development Council of America, 1973.

---

2. Theodore Roethke, "The Waking." Louis Untermeyer, ed., *Modern American Poetry* (New York: Harcourt, Brace & World, 1964), p. 599.

Recycle

by Iris Feldman

Everyone has seen a young child presented with an elaborate toy and watched him quickly tire of it and proceed to spend many happy hours with its packaging. One need only recall this familiar scene to become aware of the value of discarded material in children's play. If we begin by recognizing play as the means by which children learn about their world, then anything that has the potential to foster this learning becomes a toy. Objects to touch, look at, listen to, and "play" with provide an invitation to action and a possible experience for learning. This understanding of the value of play, and a broadened interpretation of what constitutes a toy, lead directly and naturally to the use of found, discarded, and scrounged material. What a happy situation when satisfying children's needs for toys also considers limitations of budget and the ecologically sound policy of recycling discards.

Some of the inherent qualities of discarded material make it a particularly valuable resource for children. Of prime importance is the open-ended, unstructured nature of a discard—one of Fitzhugh Dodson's criteria for evaluating a good toy. In addition to the traditional requirements that a toy be safe, durable, and provide long term fun for children, Dodson asserts that a good toy is one in which "90% of the play is in the child and 10% of the play is in the toy."[1] Thus, the proverbial box, the carton which held the toy, suggests endless possibilities for youngsters. "The box is abstract rather than specific, so it can be many things—a boat, a fort, an igloo, a submarine, an airplane, a robot. It stimulates and enriches a child's power of inventiveness."[2] Such ma-

---

1. Fitzhugh Dodson, *How to Parent* (Plainview, N.Y.: Nash Publishing Corp., 1970), p. 302. Copyright © 1970 by Dr. Fitzhugh Dodson, by permission of Nash Publishing Corporation.
2. Dodson, *How to Parent,* p. 303. Copyright © 1970 by Dr. Fitzhugh Dodson, by permission of Nash Publishing Corporation.

Iris Feldman is the librarian in the Lawrence Elementary School, Brookline, Massachusetts.

terial grants children the opportunity to work out their own play needs. It is this process that promotes self-confidence, creativity, and learning as products of play activities. What a contrast to many manufactured toys where more thought has been devoted to the commercial success of the item than to its play value. Such toys limit the play experience to a single purpose, calling for one structured response. Is it any wonder that children prefer the large cardboard box to its contents?

On still another level, toys made from found items provide additional stimulus for parent-child interaction. Parents, as the first teachers of children, can more easily become involved in the education of their children when they are aware that pots and pans, crumpled newspaper, and wooden spoons are potential teaching materials. As children grow older, the joint effort of parents and children to transform a scrap into a wonderful toy can provide the basis for a special sharing experience that transcends the simpler act of supplying a store-bought toy.

Finally, this open-ended material will adjust to meet the needs of children at various stages of development—another reason to look at discards as possible play material. This process, then, becomes much more than a token effort to offer resources to young children. It becomes a positive exploration into the world of "beautiful junk."

Infant Exploration

Studies in child development clearly indicate that the degree to which children reach their potential level of intelligence depends greatly on the amount of sensory stimulation provided before the age of five. The message here is clear: it is never too early to begin the fun of recycling discards. Clean pieces of cloth to crumple or chew on may be given to infants. Cellophane makes a delightful noise when crumpled. Plastic bottles are fine for grasping, banging, and handling. Toys made from aluminum foil, paper, cardboard, and buttons can be hung over a crib for visual stimulation. Aluminum pie plates with holes punched in them can be hung over a light or in a window to provide visual stimulation for infants as they focus on light shining through the holes. Infant gloves, made by cutting off the toe of an old sock and cutting a hole for the baby's thumb, would help infants recognize that their flailing hands do indeed belong to them. Dodson suggests sewing household materials of different textures onto a rubber pad, as in a patchwork quilt, to create a Texture Pad.[3] As the infant moves from one part of the Texture Pad to another, he experiences a changing sensory environment.

As children grow out of infancy, and their ability to sit up and coordinate eye-hand movements develops, the processes of "putting in" and "taking out" become important play activities. A trash can of discarded letters and junk

---

3. Dodson, *How to Parent,* p. 58.

mail, or a large, wide-topped plastic bottle filled with appropriate household items can function as ideal toys for children at this stage of development.

Once young children learn to control their toilet functions, water play becomes an important means of satisfying their need to "mess." The kitchen sink or the bathtub are appropriate play areas, and plastic containers, sponges, bowls, an eggbeater, straws, and perhaps even doll's clothes to wash become marvelous toys. How about allowing children to paint on the sidewalk with water and a large paint brush?

Manipulative Play

Two-year-olds, not yet able to express their feelings in words, need the opportunity for non-verbal expression in activities using crayons, paint, and clay. Recipes for art materials such as paste, finger paint, clay, and playdough are found in books of activities for children, magazine and journal articles, and even on some commercial packages. Parents find these homemade products inexpensive and useful; children are often allowed to share in their preparation. Soap bubbles are always popular. The needed solution can be made easily by mixing gently small amounts of water and liquid detergent in a shallow pan. Bubbles may be made by dipping a variety of objects in the solution. Straws, funnels, spools, mason jar rings, and, of course, young hands work beautifully. A gentle waving of the object or blowing through it will produce bubbles par excellence, and at the same time develop the child's manipulative skills. Experienced mothers recommend making flour paste with *boiling* rather than cold water for greater durability. One mother who is enthusiastic about the use of finger paint, mixes food coloring with liquid starch and allows her two children to paint pictures on the inside of the bathtub. Clean-up is easy! For playdough that remains pliable through many uses, this same mother uses a recipe that includes cooking oil and directions to cook the mixture a short time. Of course, storage in a tight container between uses is necessary.

A homemade busy board offers another opportunity to develop manipulative skills. Simply mount hardware fixtures such as hinges, handles, and a chain lock on a brightly painted board. The manipulation of these objects will keep children's hands busy and challenged.

A puzzler box that requires children to fit each of three different objects through the appropriate hole is easily made from a sturdy cardboard box. The objects could include an envelope, a cough drop box, and a section of cardboard tubing. The adult need only cut the corresponding shape in the lid. The puzzle box should be easily opened and closed to encourage the child to push the objects through the appropriate opening again and again.

Developing the Senses

Discarded items work particularly well in activities that stimulate children's developing senses. Small covered metal film cans filled with various noise-producing materials such as beads, rice, and water can serve as "sound cans" when shaken. If two sets of these cans are made, youngsters can begin to compare sounds and determine if sounds are the same or different.

An exciting guessing game stimulating the sense of touch can be played with a "feely bag," "touch box," or similar device. Scrap items of various textures such as pieces of carpet, ribbon, and corrugated cardboard must be identified by children through their sense of touch. Even very young children will have a good time experiencing these different textures. Scrapbooks of wallpaper and fabric samples also make excellent touch-and-feel books.

Pictures cut from old magazines can produce additional scrapbooks that illustrate colors, shapes, and spatial relationships. This kind of activity encourages visual discrimination and conceptual development.

It is even possible to make color scopes, a variation of the kaleidoscope, by melting crayon chips between sheets of wax paper, and covering the end of a cardboard tube with the transparent result. Children can hold the tube up to a light or in front of a window and identify the colors. Additional color scopes can be made to help children recognize new colors.

An Expansive Learning Environment

The possibilities for recycling discards are limitless for preschool children age three to five. These children are eager to make things. The combination of their active imaginations, interested parents, and a variety of found materials creates a stimulating learning environment. It is always a good idea to have a "stuff box" handy. Often the mere presence of a collection of scrounged items can stimulate exploration of the materials and the invention of a toy. Dianne Warner lists over 150 suggested pieces of "beautiful junk,"[4] but a standard collection would include tubes, milk cartons, egg cartons, empty thread spools, aluminum pans, styrofoam trays, fabric scraps, paper bags, magazines, plastic containers, yarn, buttons, paper plates and cups, boxes of all kinds, and of course old clothes. The contents of the "stuff box" is limited only by considerations of safety. Caution should be exercised to avoid objects small enough for very young children to choke on, as well as objects having sharp or rusty edges, those painted with lead-based paint, and those that might shatter. Milk and food containers should be washed out carefully.

It might be fun to consider the range of possible creations from one given item, milk cartons, for example. A set of hollow blocks for stacking or building can be made from milk cartons by cutting off the sloping tops of two cartons and slipping one inside another. The cartons may be cut down to various sizes, stuffed with crumpled newspaper for added weight, and painted or covered with contact paper. A bit of scouring powder added to the paint will

4. Dianne Warner and Jeanne Quill, *Beautiful Junk* (U.S. Dept. of Health, Education, and Welfare; Office of Child Development, Bureau of Child Development Services. Washington, D.C.: U.S. Govt. Printing Office, 1973), p. 11.

help it adhere to the smooth surface of the milk carton. A boat which will really sail can be made from an empty milk carton. Beginning at the point of the pouring spout, cut in a straight line to the bottom of the carton and then along the bottom of the carton, thus allowing the carton to open lengthwise. It will now float on the side opposite the long cut. The "boat" may be shaped as desired with sails (perhaps a paper plate), flag, or other accouterments added according to whim. Watch it go in a pool or bathtub! Patterns are available for making various pieces of doll furniture from milk cartons. And what about a train children make for themselves from milk cartons, tied together with cord and decorated with buttons, cardboard tubes, and spools. Only a train made from shoe boxes could equal the fun of a milk carton train.

Empty cans that nest inside each other for easy storage provide another stackable toy. Rough edges should be flattened with pliers, and numbers could be painted on the cans with nail polish, indicating the smallest to the largest size. Of course, children may choose to use the cans for their putting-in and taking-out play as well.

Pull toys are easily made from the round cartons in which ice cream, oatmeal, or salt are packaged. Place some beans, bottle caps, or pebbles inside the carton to create a rattle when the toy is pulled, and string a long cord through the carton and its cover.

Consider for a moment the adaptability of empty thread spools for growing, learning children. Toddlers can have a clattering pull toy if a few spools are threaded on a long string. As small muscle coordination develops, they can string the empty spools themselves, perhaps adding straws or macaroni for variety. Older children can create figures from three spools stacked on a pencil, and may even play a game by mixing the head, body, and feet portions of the spool people.

Egg cartons, too, have applications for children at various stages of development. The youngest children may use them just as they are to open and close, put in and take out, and stack as they would building blocks. Older children can decorate the box as a storage chest for their treasures. Parents can adapt the egg carton to form a teaching game by coloring each cup a different color and asking the child to match colored pieces of cardboard with the appropriate cup. Line the cups with aluminum foil to create a paint dish, or turn the carton upside down to use the inverted cups as a scissor rack. Once you realize how many ways an egg carton can be used, you'll never again throw one away.

Plastic margarine tubs lend themselves very well to the toddlers' pleasure in stacking or nesting objects. Four- or five-year-olds can create a margarine tub family. A head, tail, arms, and legs can be cut from paper and arranged in the lid. By snapping the tub into the lid the paper pieces will be held in place. The tub can then be decorated to form a creature's body. A family of these margarine tub animals can be suspended from a wire hanger to form an unusual mobile.

Parent/Child Interaction

Artistic Crafts

Styrofoam meat trays, as well as bits of styrofoam packing material, may be used in imaginative constructions, collage pictures, or printing with paint. With help from parents, these trays make ideal number cards and flash cards, sewing cards, and simple puzzles. Older children may want to pattern an airplane or a boat out of the styrofoam tray.

The young child's ability to express himself artistically can manifest itself in a variety of forms. Mobiles can be made from almost anything. Children can be encouraged to cover a wire coat hanger with crepe paper. Straws, walnuts, paper clips, discarded cookie cutters, or clothespins can be suspended from the hanger. Collage pictures similarly call for an unlimited assortment of scrap. Cloth, paper, yarn, rick-rack, and buttons may be pasted onto cardboard. Found materials from outdoors such as seeds, leaves, grasses, and wildflowers are an additional supply source. These nature items can be arranged between two sheets of wax paper, and with help from parents, the wax paper can be melted with an iron to create a transparent effect. Children can derive a real sense of achievement from such an attractive product.

A most exciting experience for children can be provided by recycling discards into living, growing gardens. A jar lid filled with water serves as a suitable growing container for the tops of carrots, onions, turnips, and pineapple. Try planting stringbeans or lentil beans in a cake pan lined with wet paper towels. A water jar and toothpicks are all that is required to grow a plant from sweet potatoes, beets, onions, or garlic; and a wet sponge curled around the inside of a glass or jar will enable young eyes to watch seeds sprout between the glass and the sponge. A terrarium can be maintained in a plastic bottle by cutting off the narrow top, placing stones in the bottom for drainage, adding enough soil to cover the stones well, and digging up a section of weeds or moss to place in the container. The ever-available egg cartons and milk cartons are also excellent planters.

Individual Interests

Combine imagination, effort, and lots of throwaways to furnish a rhythm band for young children. A coffee can with its plastic lid is a natural drum. Children may wish to decorate the can or attach a string to it so it will serve as a marching drum as well. A tambourine is easily made from two paper plates, or, for a different sound, two foil pie pans. Beans, pebbles, macaroni, or buttons can be placed inside the pans or plates to supply the sound. The plates can be taped or laced together, and then decorated with streamers if the children choose. Fill a juice can or cardboard tube with some "rattly" objects, cover the ends with foil, and children have maracas to shake. That reliable cardboard tube serves as a humming flute when holes are punched in it with a pencil and one end is covered with wax paper. Young children will enjoy blowing through the open end, fingering the holes to produce their own melodic tones.

What could be simpler than bells made by banging a spoon and a pencil together, or a kazoo made by blowing through the teeth of a comb covered with wax paper? Finger cymbals can be made from the lids of baby-food jars. Pierce two holes near the center of each lid. Thread a short piece of elastic through each pair of holes and tie the ends to form a loop. Children can fit their small fingers through the elastic and tap the lids together to produce a gentle clattering sound. To emphasize that no idea is too absurd, consider twisting rubberbands around a bottle cap to create an ear harp. The children will enjoy plucking the strings right near their ears to hear the soft sounds produced. Finally, no band would be complete without an original shoe box and cardboard tube banjo, the strings supplied, of course, by rubberbands of varying thicknesses.

These are but a few suggestions possible for projects on a musical theme. Each activity promotes the development of children's rhythmic, auditory, and coordination abilities.

The World of Make-Believe

The critical role of pretending and of involvement in the world of make-believe deserves careful consideration here. Open-ended, unstructured, scrounge material gives children an opportunity to work through their fantasies and test their perceptions of reality in the safe, accepting process of play. A collection of grown-up clothes, old hats, ties, pocketbooks, shoes, jewelry, eyeglass frames, and empty make-up accessories are a clear invitation for children to pretend being adults. A spool wrapped in aluminum foil and tied onto a string can be a stethoscope for a make-believe doctor. Cardboard tubes forced into each other and trimmed with a cardboard star become a magic wand. An imaginative, attractive hobby horse is an additional prop for pretending and can be created from paper bags to form the head, and cardboard tubes for the body.

Puppets, dolls, costumes, and masks similarly encourage children to satisfy their need to pretend. Recycled discards come in handy for these projects. A paper bag becomes the head of a doll if it is decorated, stuffed with newspaper, twisted shut, and pushed into a plastic-bottle body. Attached to a cardboard tube, this same head becomes the start for a puppet. Cut holes in a large paper bag for a child's head and arms, and you have a fine beginning for a costume. In the same way, to make a mask simply cut holes for eyes in a smaller paper bag.

Youngsters, of course, can decide for themselves the character of their costumes or masks. Puppets and other people can be created from clothespins, old socks, mittens, and gloves. Construction paper taped onto a popsicle stick or a decorated cardboard tube can also become a character in children's pretending. Plastic bottles often resemble a human figure and can be decorated to form all sorts of dolls. Rubbing the plastic bottle with sandpaper will give a more suitable drawing surface. Small children will enjoy using finger puppets made by poking holes in rubber or styrofoam balls to fit their own fingers. Material from the "stuff box" can supply the makings of faces.

Of course puppeteers often want to work from a stage, a need that can also be met by scrounge material. A large box, opened on one side, with a square cut out of the back works very effectively. The puppeteers can sit behind the box on the floor. Or if no box is available, children may just want to kneel behind a couch or large chair. Some scrap material or an old sheet or a blanket can serve as a curtain for the puppet stage.

Library Models

The validity of using scrounged material with young children should be clear, and many ideas have been suggested to demonstrate the unlimited potential of this resource. The unanswered question is: How can those who work in libraries help parents use discards found around the home as resources for learning and as stimuli for parent-child sharing?

As a good first step, librarians can set the example by using discards in their own programming for young children. The involvement of children in the world of make-believe provides a natural tie-in, because books are so often used to open the doors to this world. The strategies already described for making costumes, masks, puppets, and props can be used to encourage children to role play favorite characters or favorite stories.

After sharing a story in the library, the youngsters might be supplied with an assortment of discarded scraps to use to express their feelings, reactions to, and impressions of the story. The children may wish to represent some portion of the story in a diorama, a shadow box, or a picture made from the scrap items. Perhaps the little people's area in the library could be decorated with these projects so others would be inspired by their efforts. Library visits can also be a good time for boys and girls to make their own books by cutting up old magazines, pasting selected pictures onto construction paper, and binding their work together. These books may be enjoyed by the children themselves, or shared with other youngsters.

A flannel board can be made by stretching felt over any board. Figures may be cut from felt or from the pictures in discarded books. The paper pictures will adhere to the flannel board if they are rubbed on the back with sandpaper or pasted onto pieces of felt. These felt story boards may help the child listen to stories in the library and even tell his own stories.

Libraries on a limited budget may wish to supplement their furnishings for young children by using unusual discards. Comfortable seating for listening to stories and looking at picture books can be provided by large carpet samples, readily obtained free or for a minimal fee from carpet shops. Pillows made from fabric scraps or terry washcloths stuffed with old stockings create additional soft, comfortable surfaces. Small barrels, without their tops and bottoms, lined with carpet scraps and covered with wallpaper, become small spaces that invite children to curl up inside with a book. Consider contacting the telephone company for discarded cable spools which, when covered with oilcloth or any appealing surface, make ideal child-size tables. Marinas and boat rental facilities often dispose of old boats that are no longer seaworthy; such discards furnish another delightful space for a child's reading pleasure. Storage needs may be met by using stacked fruit crates that have been sanded, nailed together, and painted to function as shelving space.

A Continuing Quest for Ideas

To further encourage the use of discards in parent-child play activities, the library might use display space in the adult as in the children's room to highlight recycling projects. Samples of some of the projects suggested could be made and exhibited in a display case. Perhaps the exhibit could focus on uses for a discarded milk carton or on the extensive rhythm band devised from scrap. The display could be supplemented by a list of resources to consult for additional ideas.

Professional magazines for teachers such as *Early Years, Instructor, Teacher,* and *Learning* often focus on activities for very young children incorporating scrap material. Many women's magazines contain similar articles in their attempt to reach parents. Often these ideas appear as possible gifts for children to make. Some children's magazines, too, include sections of craft ideas, and parents can be encouraged to select those appropriate for very young children. *Pack o' Fun,* a magazine devoted exclusively to the art of scrap craft, can be brought to parents' attention. Libraries may want to clip pertinent articles from old periodicals and maintain a "Recycling Discards" idea file. It's also a good idea to build up the book and pamphlet material on this subject in anticipation of requests from parents, day-care center workers, and teachers working with young children. Bibliographies of these resources can be distributed. The resources cited at the conclusion of this section can be a small beginning in this effort. Again, in promoting ideas for parent-child interaction, it's important to remember the facilities of the adults' as well as the children's area of the library may be utilized.

On a broader level, those of us working in libraries can go beyond programming, displays, and building our resource collection, and publicize the efforts of other community organizations involved in collecting and redistributing discards. Publicity can be given to scout groups, community centers, day care centers, Head Start programs, and religious groups involved in recycling activities or in need of particular items. In the Boston area, for example, libraries might wish to inform parents and other adults working with young children of the efforts of the Children's Museum. This facility maintains a recycling center in which a small fee is paid for the opportunity to cart away bags of unusual material. In addition, recycling workshops are offered to suggest ways to use these materials with children. Teacher training institutions may offer similar workshops, often open to members of the community. Libraries can supplement their own resources by serving as a clearinghouse for this type of information.

If the need, personnel, and the facility permit, perhaps the library itself could become a demonstration center for the collection and redistribution of discards, as a means of encouraging other organizations to take over this activity.

Thus, despite limited funds, young children's need for play material can be met very effectively by scrounging discarded items and revitalizing them with imagination, care, and some effort. Here is an opportunity for librarians to exercise their particular ability to facilitate interaction between people and ideas. They can create an awareness of the need for recycling activities and then contribute in some way to its satisfaction—by offering suggestions, supplying information resources, or using the ideas and strategies in their own work with children. In this way they can make good use of their ability to reach parents, and through them their children, during the crucial years of development.

Bibliography

Caney, Steven. *Steven Caney's Toy Book.* New York: Workman Publishing Co., 1972.

Cole, Ann, et al. *I Saw a Purple Cow and 100 Other Recipes for Learning.* Boston: Little, Brown & Co., 1972.

Dodson, Fitzhugh. *How to Parent.* Plainview, N.Y.: Nash, 1970.

Far West Laboratory for Educational Research and Development. *A Guide to Securing and Installing the Parent/Child Toy-Lending Library.* Washington, D.C.: U.S. Govt. Printing Office, 1972.

Friends of the Perry Nursery School. *The Scrap Book: A Collection of Activities for Preschoolers.* Ann Arbor, Mich.: Friends of Perry School, 1972.

Ladner, Mildred. "From Trash to Treasure," *The National Observer,* November 9, 1974, p. 11.

Sattler, Helen Roney. *Kitchen Carton Crafts.* New York: Lothrop, Lee & Shepard, 1970.

U.S. Dept. of Health, Education, and Welfare; Office of Human Development, Office of Child Development, Children's Bureau. *Fun in the Making.* Washington, D.C.: U.S. Govt. Printing Office, 1973.

Warner, Dianne, and Jeanne Quill. *Beautiful Junk.* U.S. Dept. of Health, Education, and Welfare; Office of Child Development, Bureau of Child Development Services. Washington, D.C.: U.S. Govt. Printing Office, 1973.

Yurchak, Mary Jane, comp. *Toy List.* Brookline, Mass.: Early Education Project, 1973.

PART 3

Experiencing Literature

To the storyteller yesterday is still here. . . .
In stories time does not vanish.
Neither do men and animals. . . .
What happened long ago is still present.

Isaac Bashevis Singer
Zlateh the Goat and Other Stories, Foreword

First Steps: Storytime with Young Listeners

by Spencer G. Shaw

Storytime with young listeners may bring together children and a librarian, a teacher, a recreational leader, or a parent in many different, delightful locations. Enraptured children may gather before the book-lined shelves of a library, sit in a quiet, special "library corner" of a classroom or under the shade of trees, or lie nestled comfortably in bed. No matter what the setting, the ingredients for storytime remain the same: a storyteller, a story, and an audience.

Free for the moment from questioning adults, and emotionally and mentally liberated, each child may discover many things when books are shared: *happiness,* to release uninhibited laughter and rhythmic responses of small bodies; *wonder,* to foster fresh, childlike speculations as the stories unfold; *self-discovery,* to permit visual and mental explorations far removed from reality; *quiet solitude,* to offer a retreat from the frenetic pace of seemingly endless activities. "In solitude," said Samuel Johnson, "we have our dreams to ourselves, and in company we agree to dream in concert."[1] Children may uncover *companionship,* to be found in a group experience or in having shared identity with a fictional counterpart or with a storyteller who does not acknowledge any disparity between ages; *budding understanding,* to ex-

---

1. Samuel Johnson, "The Idler," No. 32.

Spencer G. Shaw, Associate Professor in the School of Librarianship, University of Washington, is a teacher and an authority in the fields of library service to children, library materials for children, library service to the exceptional, ethnic minority materials, and folk literature and storytelling.

cite young minds to stretch into the unknown and the new; *creativity*, to encourage little tongues to try out unfamiliar words, little hands to mold symbolic images into objective realities. The storyteller may distill and reinforce the concepts expressed by Evelyn Wenzel, who stated, "out of books creatively experienced in early childhood emerge the most permanent memories of later years."[2]

Understanding and Interacting with Children

If girls and boys are to gain these rich rewards, a storyteller must be able to look upon each young listener as a composite of many children, to respect the individuality of each child, and to reaffirm the belief that each child has potential, a capacity for growth, and a need to reach out and to be reached. Such insights will enable a storyteller

To be aware of the individuality of each child's response to a story told, an activity engaged in, or to any segment of a storytelling program

To accept that children have their own peculiar sensitivities that make them respond differently to different things and to different people

To be alert to any overt and, occasionally, covert clues a child may give in a group to indicate his feelings

To accept a child "where he is" at a particular stage of development and not where one expects the youngster to be. (All children do not reach the desired norm at the same time nor at the same rate of development.)

To understand some of the elemental fears of preschool children and to help them overcome these crises by gradual steps—especially the fears of facing a new group, listening to a particular story, or viewing a particular illustration

To learn about the backgrounds and experiences of the children in the group, to know intellectual and social levels, limitations in language and verbal skills

To understand the vulnerability of children growing up with some physical, social, or cultural differences that make it difficult for them to adjust to situations or to people; to be supportive but not overly protective in helping them achieve within these limitations

To respect each child's "value system," which may be different from that of the teller or of the others in the group

To offer a variety of opportunities that may affect individual responses in the sensory, cognitive, and affective spheres

2. Evelyn Wenzel, "Relating Creative Experience in Literature," in Leland Jacobs, ed., *Using Literature with Young Children* (New York: Teachers College Press, 1965), p. 34.

To bolster self-esteem with continuous praise—individually, by name, and as a group—for successfully participating in every phase of a storytelling program.

A storyteller needs to let each child "step to the music which he hears; however measured or far away."[3] Permit children to sense danger as the troll challenges *The Three Billy Goats Gruff* or the wolf converses with *Little Red Riding Hood*. Satisfy their love for action by racing imaginatively with *The Pancake* or plodding along in the contest between *The Hare and the Tortoise*. A storyteller needs to share listeners' responses to moments of frustration in *Alexander and the Terrible, Horrible, No Good, Very Bad Day* or when *Nobody Listens to Andrew*. Encourage children's insatiable curiosity by exploring the mystery of *Where Does the Butterfly Go When It Rains?* Invite participation in *Count and See* or adventure in *Over in the Meadow*. Offer opportunities to applaud success when Peter learns to *Whistle for Willie;* nurture the elemental desire to own possessions like *William's Doll* or Momo's *Umbrella*.

A storyteller may appeal to children's imaginations by meeting Max and sailing off to the land *Where the Wild Things Are*. Arouse their interest in other places by traveling to Paris to scamper with *Madeline* or journeying to Africa to learn to say *Jambo Means Hello* in Swahili. Offer moments to relax and ponder as children walk with the girl and her father *In the Middle of the Night;* sympathize with the children as they meet Kevin who complains *She Come Bringing Me That Little Baby Girl* or the disgruntled badger who has doubts about *A Baby Sister for Frances*. Understanding and interacting with children become prime prerequisites for a successful storytelling program.

Objectives

Once these conditions have been established, a successful preschool storytelling program is possible if a teller formulates clear, well-delineated objectives:

For a Storyteller

To share with mutual delight selected stories and poems from the field of literature for children

To stimulate the imagination

To heighten sensitivity toward living things and the natural world

For Children

To have fun and to experience happiness

To satisfy a need for play with verbal, physical, and emotional participation

To have first lessons in group experiences

---

3. *Henry David Thoreau: A Man for Our Times,* selections and drawings by James Dougherty (New York: Viking Press, 1967), p. 85.

Experiencing Literature

To guide children in the art of aural and listening comprehension

To demonstrate the importance of literature in the preschool years

To satisfy some of the basic needs and concerns of children

To bring alive authors and illustrators of children's books

To understand meanings and concepts and expand appreciation through developmental skills

To begin to have an understanding of multi-cultural, multi-ethnic environments

To recognize authors and illustrators as friends

Long-Range Planning

Long-range planning, in contrast to the day-to-day approach, provides many benefits to a storyteller. It allows time to develop a broad perspective, to read systematically and carefully, to study and analyze stories and other materials that may be included in the total program. Furthermore, this planning process gives a teller a chance to find inspiration and a chance to perfect needed skills. Time is made available, also, to enrich one's storytelling background—to acquire and assimilate knowledge of authors and illustrators, literary allusions, and a variety of facts and fantasies that broaden the teller's creative base.

Careful planning enables a storyteller to balance the selection of stories and poetry with the interests and needs of preschoolers. The program must be child-centered, the adult serving to instill and maintain interest. In this context, the words of U.S. Commissioner of Education T. H. Bell become significant:

> The great experience of early childhood is finding out that you are someone who counts in a very interesting world ... if that experience does not come in the years of early development, all later experience is likely to be tinged with a sense of futility and doubt.[4]

Furthermore, as the children develop group relationships and expand their interests, long-range planning enables a teller to adapt the program to reflect this change. Thus, when autumn heralds a new storytelling season, beginning listeners can enjoy the cumulative adventures of Danny who is told to *Ask Mr. Bear* what to give his mother for a birthday present. By spring of the following year, these same children will dare to go with Johnny Orchard into the woods to find *The Biggest Bear.*

---

4. T. H. Bell, "Early Childhood Experiences Should Concern Educators," *The National Observer,* February 22, 1975, p. 14.

Scheduling

Varied designs in scheduling have been devised for preschool storytelling programs: a weekly, year-round series; a nine-month series, beginning in September after the school year resumes and continuing through the following May; a series in segments of six to eight weeks, starting in September through to the December holidays and again from March through May; and a special series for the summer months. *Whatever plan is adopted, a preschool storytelling program must have a pattern of regularity.*

The *day* of the week, the most appropriate *time,* and the *number* of sessions per week will depend upon the community served and the extent of the other services offered by the agency where the activity is held. Some storytellers have found 10:00 A.M. to be the most suitable time, permitting mothers to return home before the lunch period begins. If the program is held in the afternoon, 1:30 P.M. is recommended to avoid conflict with the dismissal of school. Interestingly, a few agencies have experimented with a 7:30 P.M. program and publicized it as "Pajama Storytelling Time." The children are encouraged to come in bedtime attire to listen to stories as a prelude to sleep. The departure from the usual daytime scheduling of the programs makes this a unique feature.

Publicity

Once the schedule has been arranged satisfactorily, a storyteller becomes concerned with publicity. The type of formal announcements may vary, depending on the agency. *Posters* are effective and should be properly designed and professionally produced wherever possible. An attractive format is essential with good lettering, proper color combinations, and a simple, appealing picture. Include the day of the week and the time, inclusive dates, and age limits. In every instance display the poster prominently with an occasional change in location and format. Posters should be supplemented with *announcements* to parent-teacher groups and religious organizations, and *releases* to the press, radio, and TV stations. If the activity occurs in a library, *bookmarks* and *flyers* with the necessary information can be distributed at the circulation desk.

Registration

Positive community response to the publicity may make it necessary for the storyteller to plan a period of registration for children who will attend the preschool storytime. The prepared forms should include (a) the name of the child, (b) age, (c) birthday, (d) parents' names, (e) address, (f) telephone, (g) date of registration. It may be necessary to indicate the specific day when the child enrolled if there is to be more than one group of children or if the programs are in series of specified weeks. During this period of registration parents may be given a prepared booklet that contains information regarding the program and their responsibilities relating to it.

Program Content

It is important to plan a program that has a sense of *unity, balance,* and *coherence.* This is accomplished when the storyteller builds programs upon areas that interest preschool children. Some of these are bedtime, home and family, neighbors, country life, city life, daily activities, seasons, humor and nonsense, imaginary adventure, real adventure, kingdoms, castles, royalty, pets—dogs, cats, fish; birds, animals of the field and wood, wild animals, imaginary animals, sea life, zoo and circus, autos, boats, planes, trains, cowboys, minority children, peer group and sibling relationships, holidays, sights and sounds, words, letters, numbers, shapes and sizes, colors, community helpers, regions of America, other countries, Mother Goose, illustrated folk and fairy tales. A storyteller can develop any one of these interest areas through a carefully chosen *theme* that becomes the central idea to leave in the listener's mind. A properly conceived theme gives to teller and audience a sense of direction. For the narrator it facilitates the selection of material. For the listeners, the theme provides the expansion of limited concepts.

Successful preschool storytelling programs have evolved around such themes as:

The Dolls' Tea Party	Snowy Days
We All Have Birthdays	Celebrate the Circus
Let's Talk to Animals	Bedtime-Wakeup Time
Rabbits Here and There	Noisy-Quiet Storytime
Adventures with Bears	Mother Hubbard's Cupboard
Christmas Is a-Coming	A Day at the Beach
Monkeys Galore	Over in the Meadow, What Do I Find?
Mice Are Nice	When I Grow Up
A-Travelling We Will Go	On My Block, What Do I Do?
Sing Along, Sing Along	Is It Easy, Is It Hard?
Let's Go to the Farm	It's Counting Time

Literature for Storytelling Programs

Selecting the right materials for the right moment requires sensitivity and understanding. For this age group a program planner turns to picture books with their well-executed illustrations and robust texts. The discerning teller will realize that these books have a gradation in difficulty which makes some more suitable for the younger child while others have an appeal for older preschool listeners. Further, picture books can be classified in different categories: *concept books* which relate to shapes, sizes, colors, signs, letters, numbers;

picture story books in which there are well-defined plots and characterization; books to help create a *mood* or *feeling; participation books* which lead to group involvement; *textless picture books* from which stories may be created by following the characters through sequentially arranged illustrations. With a careful blend of all types, a teller can structure exciting, appealing, diverse programs. A sampling of the many titles in each category illustrates the possibilities:

Concept Books

Sparkle and Spin, a Book about Words, Ann Rand
The Very Hungry Caterpillar, Eric Carle
The House of Four Seasons, Roger Duvoisin
The Sign Book, William Duggan
Brian Wildsmith's ABC, Brian Wildsmith
Shapes and Things, Tana Hoban
Chicken Little Count-to-Ten, Margaret Friskey

Picture Story Books

Harry the Dirty Dog, Gene Zion
Swimmy, Leo Lionni
The Circus Baby, Maud and Miska Petersham
Corduroy, Don Freeman
Caps for Sale, Esphyr Slobodkina
Blueberries for Sal, Robert McCloskey
Sam, Ann H. Scott

Books to Create a Mood or Feeling

The Sleepy Book, Charlotte Zolotow
Dawn, Uri Shulevitz
Gilberto and the Wind, Marie Hall Ets
Hide and Seek Fog, Alvin Tresselt
A Book about God, Florence Mary Fitch
My Grandson Lew, Charlotte Zolotow
Seasons, John Burningham

Participation Books

It Looked like Spilt Milk, Charles Shaw
Drummer Hoff, Barbara Emberley
I Know an Old Lady, Alan Mills and Rose Bonne
But Where Is the Green Parrot?, Thomas Zacharius
Ring O' Roses, L. Leslie Brooke
Who's There? Open the Door, Bruno Munari

Experiencing Literature

Picture Books without Words

Adventures of Paddy Pork, John S. Goodall
April Fools, Fernando Krahn
A Boy, a Dog, and a Frog, Mercer Mayer
Changes, Changes, Pat Hutchins
The Good Bird, Peter Wezel
Look Again, Tana Hoban
Out! Out! Out!, Martha Alexander

Preschool programs may be further enriched with some of the simplest folktales and modern fairy tales. A number of these can be told without the aid of illustrations, permitting a listener to indulge in imaginative wanderings. However, during the past several years, many illustrated versions of traditional tales have been published for children. The storyteller must select those which have simple, uncomplicated plots. The most appealing ones are the cumulative tales with their repetitive words and phrases, such as *The Gingerbread Boy* or *The Old Woman and Her Pig.* Loving action, young listeners should hear *The Story of the Three Bears, The Wolf and the Seven Little Kids,* and continue to experience slight moments of suspense in *The Gunniwolf* or *The Turnip.* The rhythm and repetition in many simple folktales will delight preschoolers who will ask repeatedly for *Henny Penny* or echo the refrain in *The Little Red Hen* and *Millions of Cats.*

A storyteller may complement stories and picture books with the skillful use of poetry. Filled with fun, beauty, rhythm, and lyricism, well-read or well-recited poetry can spark an immediate response. A teller should blend carefully selected verse, ranging from Mother Goose and nursery rhymes to the most recent poetry collections. Excited about a discovery in the world about them—perhaps in nature—preschoolers may voice in a few words a most profound thought or a beautiful verbal image. These are the gifts a storyteller must nurture. Small children should become friends with poets through their poems. A sensitive teller may wisely accept as a talisman these words by May Hill Arbuthnot in her introduction to the book, *Time for Poetry:*

> Why then take time for poetry: Primarily, to develop a generation of children who thoroughly enjoy poetry and who can and do interpret it for themselves. But more than that, poetry can become a shining armor against ugliness, vulgarity, and brutality. The miracle of the poems... is that they take many experiences of the child's world and give them a new importance, a kind of glory that they did not have when they were just experiences.[5]

------

5. May Hill Arbuthnot, comp., "Reading Poetry to Children," in *Time for Poetry* (Chicago: Scott, Foresman & Co., 1961), p. xxiii.

Non-Book Materials
for Storytelling Programs

Alternative approaches for preschool storytelling are challenging. A story-teller must see the potential in the use of any one or a combination of multi-media components: puppets and puppetry, flannel boards, recordings, cassette tapes, films, filmstrips, and slides. However, before these are included in a program, an individual must carefully consider all of the factors related to their use. Supplementing storytelling with these components requires (a) competencies and operational skills beyond those necessary for the art form, (b) an extensive knowledge of resources and selection aids for each of the media, (c) an ability for detailed planning and preparation that combines the techniques of storytelling and utilization of the media, and (d) an understanding of how each form can add to the total learning and social experiences of the preschoolers. Multi-media components require more time in planning and preparation; however, as change agents they can be made integral parts of enriching programs for young children. Briefly analyzed, each medium has potential for preschool storytelling.

Puppetry provides a delightful extension of verbal expression as the puppets reenact the roles being described. Some storytellers have watched close friendships form between a puppet and a child. For some children who are physically or mentally handicapped or who suffer from emotional disturbances, the puppet becomes a visible, pliable character who invites needed interaction.

Flannel boards please preschoolers. They see the gradual building of a story before their eyes as a teller affixes the appropriate objects onto the flannel board while the tale is narrated. The success of this medium depends upon the skill of the storyteller in retaining a smooth delivery while handling the specially designed patterns. Occasionally, in a post-program activity, the story may be retold with the children assigned various roles and assisting the teller by adding the pictures.

Recordings and cassette tapes should relate to the program theme and reflect the mood. At no time should the operation of the equipment unduly divert the attention of the listeners. Again, the proficiency of the teller in an artistic use of records with storytelling is paramount.

Soft background music may be played as the children enter and leave a storytelling location. This helps to establish mood. Appropriate selections which have an appeal for preschoolers may be included for some of the holiday or seasonal observances. In participation activities, records may help to establish the proper rhythm, to clarify melodies and lyrics, and to give directions. Phonodiscs may complement Mother Goose rhymes and simple folksongs in picture book format: *Mommy Buy Me a China Doll, The Fox Went Out on a Chilly Night, The Old Woman and Her Pig, Go Tell Aunt Rhody,*

Frog Went a-Courtin', Old MacDonald Had a Farm, and others. Occasionally, sound recordings can be used to bring listening experiences to preschoolers if a storyteller shares a book in which there are farm animals, sea and bird life, circus or amusement park activities, traffic and harbor sounds. International understanding may be initiated with child-oriented folk music and songs from other countries.

Films, filmstrips and slides may be expertly interwoven into preschool storytime. Balanced properly within a program, they supplement but do not supplant the storytelling. If the latter occurs, the activity assumes a different character and becomes a film or filmstrip program. A teller facilitates the transitional element in the program by guiding young listeners with a suitable introduction.

A rich background knowledge of book and non-book materials for program content is essential. The storyteller acquires knowledge by the use of excellent reference and bibliographical sources. Suggestions for picture books, folktales and poetry are included in *Picture Books for Children,* edited by Patricia J. Cianciolo; *How to Conduct an Effective Picture Book Program: A Handbook,* compiled by Joanna Foster; *Reading with Your Child through Age Five,* compiled by the Child Study Association of America. Many libraries have also developed helpful lists of appropriate stories to tell.

Well-loved picture books and illustrated fairy tales have been made successfully into films and filmstrips by film makers who wisely chose to preserve the original texts and illustrations. Guides for the selection of these materials may be found in the book *A Multimedia Approach to Children's Literature,* compiled and edited by Ellin Greene and Madalynne Schoenfeld. In addition, many large library systems have lists of carefully previewed films and filmstrips that may be used in preschool programming.

Arrangement of Program Content

After the storytime material has been selected and arranged in the order of its presentation in a program, the storyteller plans an appropriate introduction and conclusion for the activity. A well-planned introduction helps to set the stage for what is to follow. Short but not too abrupt, the introduction provides a means for the listeners' ears to become attuned to the sound and level of the storyteller's voice. It helps to establish a receptive emotional climate; it fosters anticipation, expectation, curiosity. Some tellers encourage a limited time period for the sharing of an experience or the showing of a toy animal or doll which a child may have brought. When the group is meeting for the first time, welcoming each child or having the children introduce themselves by first name may help to erase initial fears. One way to encourage the release of the last "wiggles" from small bodies is to lead the group in a nursery song.

Leading the children from these pre-storytime concerns into the actual

content of the program may be achieved by means of a candlelighting ceremony. As quietness descends upon the group, the storyteller may quote a
short verse that relates to the occasion:

Story candle burning bright,
Light our path with friendly light!
Guide us on our merry way
To lands of wonder, joy, and play!
(Spencer G. Shaw)

When the last story has been told and the teller concludes with a few
words, the program can end with the ceremony of extinguishing the candle.
This ritual never fails to hold the attention of young listeners.

Within the confines of preschool storytelling programs, there is a need to
allow for a change of pace to relieve the tension of sitting, viewing, and listening. Little children have short attention spans; their interests change rapidly
and abruptly. Thus, one should plan appropriate activities between the stories,
activities that supplement program content. Group participation should be
limited to easy finger plays and simple stretching rhymes. Ring games and
party songs that require much physical exertion may overstimulate small children who will have difficulty settling down again for story listening.

Many activity ideas for finger plays and simple stretching rhythms may be
located in such books as *Let's Do Fingerplays* by Marion Grayson; *Finger
Plays and Action Rhymes* by Frances Jacobs; *Finger Plays* by Emilie Poulsson;
Juba This and Juba That by Virginia Tashjian; *This Little Pig Went to Market*
by Norah Montgomerie; and *Singing Days of Childhood: Songs, Poems, Finger Plays and Rhythms for the Young Child* by Florence Ray.

Post-Program Activities

Post-program activities are important follow-ups to what has occurred: creative dramatics based on some of the stories or poems which were shared in
the program; arts and crafts to provide outlets for the preschoolers and give
further dimensions to their viewing and listening skills; reading guidance to
suggest to parents materials to use in a home setting. These post-program activities also demand a different pace and may upset the rhythmic balance that
has been carefully nurtured for storytelling. They should be a separate entity
with the storyteller using the contents of the program as a springboard to
guide and motivate the children into these other areas of creativity.

Summary of Program Planning

Putting together all of the components of a preschool storytime program,
the following plan is suggested:

Experiencing Literature

Number of children per group: 15–20 (If 30 or more, divide into two groups.)

Length of Program: 20–25 minutes (depending on attention span)

Program Design:

Introduction: Show-and-Tell, Nursery Song or Finger Play, Welcoming New Children

Opening: Candlelighting ceremony/Quoting a short verse, Brief exploration of theme

Listening Time: Introducing and telling first story

Activity Time: Carefully taught and properly guided finger play

Listening Time: Introducing and telling second story, or screening a film or filmstrip

> *Optional:* The following two components to be used before closing if time permits:

> *Activity Time:* Repeat same finger play or use poetry or nursery rhymes

> *Listening Time:* Introducing and telling a story

Closing: Repeating titles and authors of books which were used, Ceremony of extinguishing the candle

Browsing Time: Distributing books, Sharing ideas with children and parents

Preparation

A teller must give some thought to establishing the proper setting to create an atmosphere that contributes to listening. The area selected should be free of distractions. The setting must not be too limiting in size nor so large that a sense of closeness and intimacy is lacking. The location should be clean, attractive, and orderly. Cluttered furniture, sandboxes, temporarily abandoned toys and other nursery school accessories should be removed.

An informal semicircular seating arrangement should be provided. This permits the storyteller to maintain eye contact with each child and also facilitates the showing of illustrations with "...children's faces looking up/Holding wonder like a cup."[6]

A wise storyteller recognizes individual differences among children and maintains good eye contact with each one throughout the program. This device helps foster inclusiveness. How eagerly preschoolers react may also depend on the storyteller's facial expressions. A thought attributed to Alexander Smith, nineteenth-century Scottish writer, poetically calls attention to the significance of facial expressions: "If we could but read it, every human being

---

6. Sara Teasdale, "Barter," in Helen Ferris, comp., *Favorite Poems Old and New* (Garden City, N.Y.: Doubleday & Co., 1957), p. 21.

carries his life in his face. On our features the fine chisels of thought and emotion are eternally at work."

If the floor is carpeted, children may be invited to sit on the carpet. Individual plastic mats or rug-sample squares can also be used for seating. Oversized chairs are uncomfortable for little children and should be avoided. Each child should have his or her own place to sit before the program begins. If the children are seated on the floor, the storyteller should sit on a low stool. When the activity is held outdoors, a shady and grassy location is best. A blanket or rug should be provided for a cement-covered area or a sandy beach.

A storyteller should establish a *focal point* in the setting. This may be a low table or a bookcase with a display of artistically arranged picture books, an appropriate artifact, or freshly cut flowers. For seasonal programs, holidays, or special occasions other suitable displays should be used. The candle used in the candlelighting ceremony can also be included in the setting.

Name tags, which are an effective means for group control, may be designed to follow the program theme. The distribution of the tags enables a storyteller to become acquainted with the children and welcome newcomers. During the program a teller may refer to the tag and quietly call a child by name to halt disturbing behavior. Following each program the name tags may be kept by the children as a reminder of the theme. If providing new tags each week is too time consuming, the tags can be collected at the end of the first program to be used in subsequent programs.

A storyteller should avoid dressing in the costume of a rabbit, clown, witch, Indian, and so forth. These character portrayals draw attention away from the stories to the teller. It is the program content that is important; the storyteller serves as a medium through whom this content is transmitted. Particular dress indigenous to the culture of a teller would be appropriate and educational for the children to see.

When picture books are shared with the listeners, one vital concern is the most suitable method for showing the illustrations. Some read the text page by page, pause, then show the illustrations. Others hold the book either to the left or to the right, reading the text and showing the accompanying pictures simultaneously. The best presentation is one where the story is learned, and the storyteller does not have to look at the words. The illustrations are shown as the story is being told. The teller masters the text by reading it both silently and aloud several times and practicing delivery of the text with the proper showing of illustrations. Initially, there will be a lack of coordination; however, with persistent work, the two elements will gradually fuse. The finished presentation will be an exciting blend of verbal and illustrative imagery. Children inevitably extract more meaning from a story presented in this manner. Perhaps they will share the feelings of Paul Hazard when he wrote:

> I like books . . . that provide them with pictures, the kind that they like; pictures chosen from the riches of the whole world; enchanting pictures that bring release and joy, happiness gained before reality closes in upon them, insurance against the time, all too soon, when there will be nothing but realities.[7]

Personal preparation also means a refinement of *speech patterns.* The storyteller must realize the importance of excellent diction and clarity. Unimaginative colloquialisms, poor sentence structure, and mutilated pronunciations rob the English language of its beauty. It is fascinating to watch little mouths trying to repeat a word that the storyteller has used. Its sound, its rhythm, and its strangeness offer a challenge to young imitators.

Presentation of the Storytime

The moment has arrived. On the appointed day the children come for their very own program. While they are gathering, the storyteller, with the help of the parents, assists them in removing their coats. Name tags are distributed, and each child is invited to browse among the picture books placed on the tables. The recorded music playing in the story area attracts the children, who wait until the storyteller guides them to the place where the program is to occur. The teller invites the children to sit down. When everyone is comfortable, the storyteller waits as an almost imperceptible lull comes over the conversation; the music is stopped and the teller speaks.

When the needed rapport is established, preschoolers and their older friend will be able to progress from one element of the program to the next. Young children respond to a teller and to a story when they recognize in both a sense of honesty. What the adult values, they value. If the storyteller reveals an enthusiasm for the story which is being shared, children will place a high premium upon the gift; if the telling is superficial and lackluster, the offering will be spurned.

The teller should sustain a proper pitch to enable each listener to hear without straining. A resonant and melodious voice will command immediate attention. The storyteller should pause at appropriate moments. The need of small listeners "to catch up" should be respected, for the children do not progress at the same pace as the storyteller. The pause will also change the pace and hint of a new direction in the story line.

A good storyteller supplements voice control with eye contact and pleasant facial expressions. Many of the preschoolers will be ready to respond to a returned look, a smile, or a word. Others may be shy, glancing downward or around, not knowing exactly what is expected of them. A few may be listless

---

7. Paul Hazard, *Books, Children and Men* (Boston: The Horn Book, 1960), p. 42.

while others are exuberant. A sensitive storyteller will recognize these differences and use eye contact to bring everyone into the group and invite participation. On a teller's face children may see warmth or aloofness, friendliness or dislike, acceptance or rejection, enthusiasm or boredom. If children see no smile as Curious George engages in his rib-tickling antics, they may miss the humor. If they do not witness a teller's concern for Peter Rabbit's plight, it will be difficult for them to empathize fully with his predicament. In this regard Chukovsky believes:

> The goal of storytellers ... consists of fostering in the child, at whatever cost, compassion and humaneness—this miraculous ability of man to be disturbed by another being's misfortunes, to feel joy about another being's happiness, to experience another's fate as one's own. Storytellers take trouble to teach the child in his early years to participate with concern in the lives of imaginary people and animals, and to make sure that in this way he will escape the narrow frame of his egocentric interests and feelings.[8]

During the actual presentation of a picture book, the teller lets the preschoolers study the pictures and make their own discoveries. Quietly remaining in the background, the narrator will nonetheless be aware of how the children are reacting emotionally and intellectually. Spontaneous responses reveal the depth of their involvement in a story. A wise storyteller will allow such personal, brief digressions to occur without interrupting them. Then, at the proper moment, the listeners may be guided on to the next segment of the story. If there is no apparent response, the teller does not engage in a fruitless "fishing expedition" to unearth reaction. Children have the right to store up any private feelings. When a story has ended, an understanding teller will refrain from asking questions to determine reactions.

Control

If emergency situations do arise, the teller should handle them in a poised and confident manner. For example, a new member of the group may begin to cry and wish to return to mother. A hyperactive youngster may become a disruptive factor. A child may refuse to sit down or prefer to sit in the storyteller's lap. A listener who requests a drink of water or the use of a lavatory may initiate a chain reaction that is difficult to stop. The unexpected appearance of an animal, a person, or even an insect may divert the children's attention. In each instance, there is no one standard procedure to follow. A storyteller

---

8. Kornei Chukovsky, *From Two to Five* (Berkeley: Univ. of California Press, 1968), p. 138.

must determine the best technique for that time with that child. Patience and understanding should be the keys that sustain the proper listening mood and storytime atmosphere. Sharp tones, displeased looks, ridicule, or efforts to shame the preschooler must be avoided.

Eventually, storytime draws to a close while the children are still interested and asking for more. A wise storyteller will not respond with more stories but will keep the magical allure for another time. In a quiet moment at the close of the session, both storyteller and listeners can reflect upon all that has gone before.

Parents

Should parents be invited to be part of the audience? Practices vary in this regard. Many storytellers object to having adults in attendance, feeling that in the presence of parents the child fails to enter fully into group activities. On the other hand, when parents attend, there is an opportunity to acquaint them with the effective use of books, the types of material children like, and creative authors and illustrators. In some communities there are too few opportunities for parents to have a shared reading experience with their child. This may be due to economic conditions, to a limited educational background, or a lack of knowledge regarding techniques. For these parents, participation in the storytelling program is invaluable.

In any event, parents should be prompt in bringing their children to storytime and remain close by while the program is in progress to be available if there is a need. They should certainly be present at the conclusion of the program to pick up the children. It is desirable for the teller to visit with the adults at this time and suggest follow-up activities in the home. Reading guidance should be given as books are selected for family use. This is also the time for a tactful discussion concerning a particular child with a behavior problem.

Evaluation

The evaluation process is a vital part of the total program. No program is complete until a storyteller critically analyzes each component. Were the expectations of the children, parents, and storyteller realized? Was the program compatible with the needs and interests of preschoolers? Was each phase completed successfully? Was the preparation satisfactory? What were the strengths and weaknesses of the presentation? Were the objectives realistic? Were they attained? What changes or alternative approaches should be considered for future programs?

The scope and depth of the evaluation will vary with each storyteller. Many use a simple record book or record cards which contain date and time; attendance; theme; the stories, poems, finger plays and songs; media utilized; evaluative comments; and the storyteller's name. A checklist of program objectives aids in placing evaluative comments in perspective.

The cycle is completed. If these first steps into storytelling are to have any significance for children in early childhood, they must be guided by a story-teller who has mastered those principles of a disciplined art-form which will lead to a level of excellence. Accepting this personal commitment, a teller, with a well-presented story, may become the needed catalyst to stimulate a young mind in its never ending quest to imagine and to probe.

Appendix: Evaluation Report—Storytelling Program

Agency: _____ Date: _____

Address: _____ Telephone: _____

Date of program: _____ Hour: _____

Program length (in time): _____

Age level of audience: _____

Attendance: _____

Theme selected for program: _____

Stories told: Titles: Source:

_____   _____

_____   _____

_____   _____

_____   _____

Poetry selected: Titles: Source:

_____   _____

_____   _____

_____   _____

_____   _____

Books displayed:

_____ _____ _____

_____ _____ _____

_____ _____ _____

_____ _____ _____

Media used:

_____ _____ _____

_____ _____ _____

_____ _____ _____

Story selection: Comment briefly in terms of—

Suitability for theme: _____

Suitability for audience: _____

Interest appeals of material: _____

Illustrations and text: _____

Experiencing Literature

Location of program: (Brief description of setting; evaluative comments.)

_____

_____

Storyteller's preparation:

_____

_____

Storyteller's presentation: Elements to consider—

Familiarity with material	Pacing	Eye contact
Voice qualities	Use of pause	Facial expressions
Diction	Interpretation	Gestures
Enunciation	Expression	Posture

Program activities: (Finger plays, Stretching exercises, Participation activities)

_____

_____

_____

Audience response:
  To stories: _____
  To poetry: _____
  To activities: _____
  To storyteller: _____
  To media: _____

Post-program activity:
  Browsing period: _____

_____

  Creative dramatics: _____

_____

  Arts and crafts: _____

_____

  Other: _____

_____

Evaluator: _____

References to Children's Books

Alexander, Martha. *Out! Out! Out!* Illus. by the author. New York: Dial Press, 1968.

Asbjörnsen, Peter C. and Moe, Jorgen E. *The Three Billy Goats Gruff.* Illus. by Marcia Brown. New York: Harcourt, Brace & World, 1957.

Association for Childhood Education International. "The Pancake," in *Told under the Green Umbrella: Old Stories for New Children.* New York: Macmillan Publishing Co., 1930.

Bemelmans, Ludwig. *Madeline.* Illus. by the author. New York: Viking Press, 1939.

Brooke, L. Leslie. "The Story of the Three Bears," in *The Golden Goose Book.* Illus. by the compiler. New York: Frederick Warne & Co., 1905.

Burningham, John. *Seasons.* Illus. by the author. Indianapolis, Ind.: Bobbs-Merrill Co., 1971.

Carle, Eric. *The Very Hungry Caterpillar.* Illus. by the author. Cleveland: World Publishing Co., 1972.

Chicken Little. *Henny Penny.* Retold and illus. by Paul Galdone. New York: Seabury Press, 1968.

Domanska, Janina. *The Turnip.* Illus. by the author. New York: Macmillan Publishing Co., 1969.

Dugan, William. *The Sign Book.* Illus. by the author. New York: Golden Press, 1968.

Duvoisin, Roger. *The House of Four Seasons.* Illus. by the author. New York: Lothrop, Lee & Shepard Co., 1956.

Emberley, Barbara. *Drummer Hoff.* Illus. by Ed Emberley. Englewood Cliffs, N.J.: Prentice-Hall, 1967.

Ets, Marie Hall. *Gilberto and the Wind.* Illus. by the author. New York: Viking Press, 1963.

Feelings, Muriel. *Jambo Means Hello: Swahili Alphabet Book.* Illus. by Tom Feelings. New York: Dial Press, 1974.

Fisher, Aileen. *In the Middle of the Night.* Illus. by Adrienne Adams. New York: Thomas Y. Crowell Co., 1965.

Fitch, Florence Mary. *A Book about God.* Illus. by Leonard Weisgard. New York: Lothrop, Lee & Shepard Co., 1953.

Flack, Marjorie. *Ask Mr. Bear.* Illus. by the author. New York: Macmillan Publishing Co., 1932.

The Fox Went Out on a Chilly Night; an Old Song. Illus. by Peter Spier. Garden City, N.Y.: Doubleday & Co., 1961.

Freeman, Don. *Corduroy.* Illus. by the author. New York: Viking Press, 1968.

Friskey, Margaret. *Chicken Little Count-to-Ten.* Illus. by Katherine Evans. Chicago: Childrens Press, 1946.

Experiencing Literature

Gag, Wanda. *Millions of Cats.* Illus. by the author. New York: Coward McCann, 1928.

Garelick, May. *Where Does the Butterfly Go When It Rains?* Illus. by Leonard Weisgard. New York: William R. Scott, 1961.

The Gingerbread Boy. Illus. by Paul Galdone. New York: Seabury Press, 1974.

Go Tell Aunt Rhody. Illus. by Aliki. New York: Macmillan Publishing Co., 1974.

Goodall, John S. *The Adventures of Paddy Pork.* Illus. by the author. New York: Harcourt Brace Jovanovich, 1968.

Greenfield, Eloise. *She Come Bringing Me That Little Baby Girl.* Illus. by John Steptoe. New York: J. B. Lippincott Co., 1974.

Grimm, Jacob. *Little Red Riding Hood; a Story by the Brothers Grimm.* Illus. by Harriet Pincus. New York: Harcourt Brace Jovanovich, 1968.

———. *The Wolf and the Seven Little Kids; a Story by the Brothers Grimm.* Illus. by Felix Hoffmann. New York: Harcourt Brace Jovanovich, 1959.

Guilfoile, Elizabeth. *Nobody Listens to Andrew.* Illus. by Mary Stevens. Chicago: Follett Publishing Co., 1957.

Harper, Wilhelmina. *The Gunniwolf.* Illus. by William Wiesner. New York: E. P. Dutton & Co., 1967.

Hoban, Russell. *Bedtime for Frances.* Illus. by Garth Williams. New York: Harper & Row, Publishers, Inc., 1960.

Hoban, Tana. *Count and See.* Illus. by the author with photographs. New York: Macmillan Publishing Co., 1972.

———. *Look Again.* Illus. by the author. New York: Macmillan Publishing Co., 1971.

———. *Shapes and Things.* Illus. by the author. New York: Macmillan Publishing Co., 1970.

Hutchins, Pat. *Changes, Changes.* Illus. by the author. New York: Macmillan Publishing Co., 1971.

Keats, Ezra Jack. *Whistle for Willie.* Illus. by the author. New York: Viking Press, 1964.

Krahn, Fernando. *April Fools.* Illus. by the author. New York: E. P. Dutton & Co., 1974.

La Fontaine, Jean de. *The Hare and the Tortoise.* Illus. by Brian Wildsmith. New York: Franklin Watts, 1967.

Langstaff, John. *Frog Went a-Courtin'.* Illus. by Feodor Rojankovsky. New York: Harcourt, Brace and World, 1955.

———. *Over in the Meadow.* Illus. by Feodor Rojankovsky. New York: Harcourt, Brace and World, 1957.

Lionni, Leo. *Swimmy.* Illus. by the author. New York: Pantheon Books, 1963.

"The Little Red Hen and the Grain of Wheat." In *Chimney Corner Stories:*

Tales for Little People, by Veronica Hutchinson. Illus. by Lois Lenski. New York: G. P. Putnam's Sons, 1925.

Mayer, Mercer. *A Boy, a Dog, and a Frog.* Illus. by the author. New York: Dial Press, 1967.

McCloskey, Robert. *Blueberries for Sal.* Illus. by the author. New York: Viking Press, 1948.

Mills, Alan, and Bonne, Rose. *I Know an Old Lady.* Illus. by Abner Graboff. Chicago: Rand McNally & Co., 1961.

Mommy, Buy Me a China Doll. Adapted from an Ozark Children's Song by Harve Zemach. Illus. by Margot Zemach. Chicago: Follett Publishing Co., 1966.

Mother Goose. *Ring O' Roses; a Nursery Rhymes Picture Book.* Illus. by L. Leslie Brooke. New York: Frederick Warne & Co., n.d.

Munari, Bruno. *Who's There? Open the Door!* Illus. by the author. Cleveland: World Publishing Co., 1957.

Old MacDonald Had a Farm. Illus. by Robert Quackenbush. New York: J. B. Lippincott Co., 1972.

The Old Woman and Her Pig. Illus. by Paul Galdone. New York: McGraw-Hill Book Co., 1960.

Petersham, Maud and Miska. *The Circus Baby.* Illus. by the authors. New York: Macmillan Publishing Co., 1950.

Potter, Beatrix. *The Tale of Peter Rabbit.* Illus. by the author. New York: Frederick Warne and Co., n.d.

Rand, Ann. *Sparkle and Spin; a Book about Words.* Illus. by Paul Rand. New York: Harcourt, Brace and World, 1957.

Rey, H. A. *Curious George.* Illus. by the author. Boston: Houghton Mifflin Co., 1941.

Scott, Ann. *Sam.* Illus. by Symeon Shimin. New York: McGraw-Hill Book Co., 1967.

Sendak, Maurice. *Where the Wild Things Are.* Illus. by the author. New York: Harper & Row, Publishers, Inc., 1963.

Shaw, Charles. *It Looked like Spilt Milk.* Illus. by the author. New York: Harper & Row, Publishers, Inc., 1947.

Shulevitz, Uri. *Dawn.* Words and pictures by the author. New York: Farrar, Straus & Giroux, 1974.

Slobodkina, Esphyr. *Caps for Sale; a Tale of a Peddlar, Some Monkeys and Their Monkey Business.* Illus. by the author. New York: William R. Scott, 1947.

Tresselt, Alvin. *Hide and Seek Fog.* Illus. by Roger Duvoisin. New York: Lothrop, Lee & Shepard Co., 1965.

Viorst, Judith. *Alexander and the Terrible, Horrible, No Good, Very Bad Day.* Illus. by Ray Cruz. New York: Atheneum Publishers, 1972.

Experiencing Literature

Ward, Lynd. *The Biggest Bear.* Illus. by the author. Boston: Houghton Mifflin Co., 1952.
Wezel, Peter. *The Good Bird.* Illus. by the author. New York: Harper & Row, Publishers, Inc., 1964.
Wildsmith, Brian. *Brian Wildsmith's ABC.* Illus. by the author. New York: Franklin Watts, 1963.
Yashima, Mitsu. *Umbrella.* Illus. by the author. New York: Viking Press, 1958.
Zacharius, Thomas and Wanda. *But Where Is the Green Parrot?* Illus. by the authors. New York: Delacorte Press, 1968.
Zion, Gene. *Harry the Dirty Dog.* Illus. by Margaret Bloy Graham. New York: Harper & Row, Publishers, Inc., 1965.
Zolotow, Charlotte. *My Grandson Lew.* Illus. by William Pene du Bois. New York: Harper & Row, Publishers, Inc., 1974.
———. *The Sleepy Book.* Illus. by Vladimir Babri. New York: Lothrop, Lee & Shepard Co., 1958.
———. *William's Doll.* Illus. by William Pene du Bois. New York: Harper & Row, Publishers, Inc., 1972.

Bibliography

STORYTELLING

Carlson, Bernice. *Listen and Help Tell the Story.* Nashville: Abingdon Press, 1965.
Child Study Association of America. *Reading with Your Child through Age Five.* New York: Child Study Association of America, latest edition.
Cianciolo, Patricia, ed. *Picture Books for Children.* Chicago: American Library Association, 1973.
———. "Use Wordless Picture Books to Teach Reading, Visual Literacy and to Study Literature," *Top of the News* 29:226–34 (April 1973).
Filstrup, J. "Children + Picture Blocks = Story Making and Telling," *Top of the News* 29:46–53 (Nov. 1972).
Fletcher, Helen T. *Fingerplay Poems for Children.* Darien, Conn.: Teachers Publishing Co., 1964.
Foster, Joanna, comp. *How to Conduct Effective Picture Book Programs; a Handbook.* New York: Westchester Library System, 1967.
Grayson, Marion. *Let's Do Fingerplays.* Washington: Robert B. Luce, 1962.
Greene, Ellin. "The Pre-School Story Hour Today," *Top of the News* 31:80–85 (Nov. 1974).
Jacobs, Frances E. *Finger Plays and Action Rhymes.* New York: Lothrop, Lee & Shepard Co., 1941.
Miller, Zajan and Mary. *Musical Finger Play.* New York: Charles Scribner's Sons, 1955.

Montgomerie, Norah. *This Little Pig Went to Market; Play Rhymes.* New York: Franklin Watts, 1967.

Moore, Vardine. *Pre-School Story Hour,* 2nd ed. Metuchen, N.J.: Scarecrow Press, 1972.

New York Library Association. *Once Upon a Time.* rev. ed. by the Picture Book Committee, Children's and Young Adult Section, New York Library Assoc. New York: New York Public Library.

Peterson, Ellin. "Pre-School Hour," *Top of the News* 18:47–51 (Dec. 1961).

Poulsson, Emilie. *Finger Plays for Nursery and Kindergarten.* New York: Dover Publications, 1971.

Ray, Florence. *Singing Days of Childhood, Songs, Poems, Finger Plays and Rhythms for the Young Child.* Minneapolis: T. S. Denison & Co., 1967.

Sawyer, Ruth. *The Way of the Storyteller.* New York: Viking Press, 1962.

Schattner, Regina. *Creative Dramatics for Handicapped Children.* New York: John Day Co., 1967.

Scott, Louise B., and Thompson, Jesse J. *Rhymes for Fingers and Flannelboards.* New York: McGraw-Hill Book Co., 1960.

Shedlock, Marie. *The Art of the Storyteller.* New York: Dover Publications, 1951.

Siks, Geraldine. *Children's Literature for Dramatization.* New York: Harper & Row, Publishers, Inc., 1964.

Tashjian, Virginia. *Juba This and Juba That; Story Hour Stretches for Large and Small Groups.* Boston: Little, Brown & Co., 1969.

Toothaker, Roy E. "Songs in Picture Book Format," *Wilson Library Bulletin* 49:295–98 (Dec. 1974).

INDEXES AND BIBLIOGRAPHICAL AIDS

Brewton, John E. and Sara W., comps. *Index to Children's Poetry: a Title, Subject, Author and First Line Index to Poetry in Collections for Children and Youth.* New York. II. W. Wilson, 1942

———— ———. *First Supplement.* 1954.

———— ———. *Second Supplement.* 1965.

———. *Index to Poetry for Children and Young People, 1964–1969.* New York: H. W. Wilson, 1972.

Cathon, Laura, et al., eds. *Stories to Tell to Children.* 8th ed.; published for Carnegie Library of Pittsburgh Children's Services. Pittsburgh: University of Pittsburgh Press, 1974.

Greene, Ellin, ed. *Stories: A List of Stories to Tell and Read Aloud,* rev. ed. New York: New York Public Library, 1965.

—— and Schoenfeld, Madalyne, comps. *A Multimedia Approach to Children's Literature: A Selective List of Films, Filmstrips, and Recordings Based on Children's Books.* Chicago: American Library Association, 1972.

Experiencing Literature

Hardendorf, Jeanne, ed. *Stories to Tell.* 5th ed. Baltimore: Enoch Pratt Free Library, 1965.

Ireland, Norma, ed. *Index to Fairy Tales, 1949–1972, Including Folklore, Legends and Myths.* Westwood, Mass.: F. W. Faxon Co., 1973.

Ziegler, Elsie B. *Folklore: an Annotated Bibliography and Index to Single Editions.* Westwood, Mass.: F. W. Faxon Co., 1973.

FILMS

The Lively Art of Picture Books. Color. 57 min. 16 mm. Narrated by John Langstaff; written and directed by Joanna Foster Dougherty; produced by Morton Schindel. Weston, Conn.: Weston Woods Studios, 1964.

The Pleasure Is Mutual: How to Conduct Effective Picture Book Programs. Color. 24 min. 16 mm. Narrated by B. Davie Napier; produced by Joanna Foster and William D. Stoneback. Westport, Conn.: Connecticut Films, 1966.

Reaching Out: the Library and the Exceptional Child. Color. 25 min. 16 mm. Produced by Joanna Foster and William D. Stoneback. Westport, Conn.: Connecticut Films, 1968.

Poetry to Please Preschoolers

by Charlotte Leonard

If it is true that little children begin to appreciate literature and art through exposure to picture books written with style and illustrated with artistic skill, it should follow then that carefully planned poetry-sharing experiences will encourage their liking for poetry. Listening to verse can add immeasurably to the literary experience of children, contribute to the development of their language skills, and increase their awareness of sights, sounds, and even smells.

Few elementary and high school teachers consider poetry a favorite form of literary expression in their classes. Isn't it sad that so many of their students will be missing the joy of poetry reading for a whole lifetime?

The *preschool* years are ideal for the introduction of poetry. Experience teaches that the love of rhythm is basic to preschoolers. How babies like to be rocked, bounced, and patted rhythmically! Infants and toddlers respond happily to rollicking selections from Mother Goose and usually react vigorously to the rhythmic motions that often accompany the rhymes. What fun to ride "horseback" on knees that keep time to the words:

> Trot, trot to Boston
> To buy a loaf of bread.
> Trot, trot home again,
> The old trot's dead.[1]

---

1. John Petersham, "Trot, Trot to Boston" in *The Rooster Crows* (New York: Macmillan Publishing Co., 1945), p. 6.

Charlotte Leonard is Coordinator of Children's Services, Dayton and Montgomery County Public Library, Dayton, Ohio.

Experiencing Literature

There are smiles and chuckles for the adult who guides the infant's hands as they share:

> Pat-a-cake, pat-a-cake,
> Baker's man!
> Make me a cake
> As fast as you can.
>
> Roll it, and roll it
> And mark it with T,
> And throw it in the oven
> For Tommy and me.[2]

When children get beyond the baby stage, they enjoy doing finger plays to accompany short action rhymes, such as:

> Here's a cup, and here's a cup,
> And here's a pot of tea.
> Pour a cup, and pour a cup,
> And have a drink with me.[3]

and

> These are Grandma's spectacles
> And here is Grandma's hat;
> And here's the way she folds her hands
> And puts them in her lap.[4]

Preschoolers enjoy listening and responding physically to the rhythm and sound of verse.

Often speaking poetically themselves, preschool children seem naturally receptive to thoughts expressed beautifully, uniquely, or humorously. Apt words and terse expressions are the very essence of poetry, and, like the poet, children learning to talk often express complex ideas with a minimum of words. Grown-ups are frequently surprised to hear quite ordinary words used in original and refreshing ways. As they build their own vocabularies, toddlers have a natural fascination with and appreciation for the sounds of words. For instance, one little girl, returning a book to the bookmobile, informed the

---

2. "Pat-a-Cake, Pat-a-Cake," in *The Real Mother Goose* (Chicago: Rand McNally, 1916), p. 14.

3. Marion F. Grayson, "Here's a Cup, Here's a Cup" in *Let's Do Fingerplays* (Washington, D.C.: Robert B. Luce, 1962), p. 83.

4. Grayson, "Grandmother's Spectacles," p. 41.

librarian that the book was "delicious." Another stated that the little boy with her was her "friend boy."

Young children delight in making up words. A little girl returning with her grandfather from a visit to a small natural history museum shared this opinion: "That was nice, but zoos are funner." Preschoolers also have a natural appreciation for the words that poets coin:

Dog means dog,
And cat means cat;
And there are lots
Of words like that.

A cart's a cart
To pull or shove,
A plate's a plate,
To eat off of.

But there are other
Words I say
When I am left
Alone to play.

Blum is one.
Blum is a word
That very few
Have ever heard.

I like to say it,
"Blum, Blum, Blum"—
I do it loud
Or in a hum.

All by itself
It's nice to sing:
It does not mean
A single thing.[5]

The ridiculous and zany have a special appeal. Children giggle and laugh over the peculiar sounds of certain words. A small visiting cousin was observed running up and down porch steps yelling "parsnips" over and over again, as if it were the funniest word in the world. An appreciation for words and the ability to respond emotionally to their sounds can be developed into a love for poetry.

Small children have bright, inquisitive eyes that shine with excitement over seeing for the first time what has long ago become commonplace to adults. Delight in observation is a must for the poet and the poetry enthusiast. Wonder and delight go together, often creating an ideal atmosphere for the introduction of a poem. A dentist who had his office in one part of his home was startled one day when his small son burst into the office with a worm—the child had never seen one before. It was certainly not like anything else he had ever encountered, and he wanted his father to share in his discovery of this strange creature. What a perfect opportunity to read:

5. Dorothy Aldis, "Blum" in *All Together* (New York: G. P. Putnam's Sons, 1952), p. 163. Reprinted by permission of G. P. Putnam's Sons. Copyright 1925–1928, 1934, 1939, 1952 by Dorothy Aldis. Copyright renewed.

Dickie found a broken spade
And said he'd dig himself a well;
And then Charles took a piece of tin,
And I was digging with a shell.

Then Will said he would dig one too.
We shaped them out and made them wide,
And I dug up a piece of clod
That had a little worm inside.

We watched him pucker up himself
And stretch himself to walk away.
He tried to go inside the dirt
But Dickie made him wait and stay.

His shining skin was soft and wet.
I poked him once to see him squirm.
And then Will said, "I wonder if
He knows that he's a worm."

And then we sat back on our feet
And wondered for a little bit.
And we forgot to dig our wells
A while, and tried to answer it.

And while we tried to find it out,
He puckered in a little wad,
And then he stretched himself again
And went back home inside the clod.[6]

It's a challenge to the poet to keep alive the ability to look at the everyday world with the preschooler's sense of wonder. It means he must keep all of his senses alert to original ways of interpreting day-to-day experiences.

Hearing poetry read is all-important to preschoolers because they cannot yet read for themselves. Of all the various types of literature, poetry more than any other cries to be read aloud. Only in reading a poem aloud can one feel the melody of the lines, appreciate fully the choice of words, and interpret the mood. The experience of sharing a poem and perhaps laughing over it makes the emotional response more intense. The preschool years, before

---

6. Elizabeth Madox Roberts, "The Worm" in *Under the Tree* (New York: Viking Press, 1950), pp. 46–47. © 1930 Elizabeth Madox Roberts.

children can read for themselves, are the most appropriate time for one-to-one poetry-listening experiences.

Authorities on child development stress that the years before children enter school are the most important of the whole life span. This is the time children are absorbing all kinds of knowledge as well as attitudes and feelings. Just learning to recognize poetry and learning that it is fun to listen to are basic concepts to build on for school and later years. It is important that children learn about the very succinct way emotions and feelings can be expressed through poetry. This background will provide motivation for further independent exploration.

Now that it has been established that preschoolers are a natural audience for poetry, what kind of verse will they like? Their instinct for rhythm and rhyme has already been discussed. Poetry with a refrain or considerable repetition is appealing also, because children like the familiar. They especially like to participate by repeating lines or verses with the reader. Poems like this offer that kind of opportunity:

> I know a little cupboard,
> With a teeny tiny key,
> And there's a jar of Lollypops
>   For me, me, me.

> It has a little shelf, my dear,
> As dark as dark can be,
> And there's a dish of Banbury Cakes
>   For me, me, me.

> And I have a small fat grandmamma,
> With a very slippery knee,
> And she's Keeper of the Cupboard,
>   With the key, key, key.

> And when I'm very good, my dear,
> As good as good can be,
> There's Banbury Cakes and Lollypops
>   For me, me, me.[7]

Little children love to laugh, and much of the poetry collected in anthologies for this age group is humorous. *Laughing Time* by William Jay Smith (Little, Brown) is a whole book of funny poems.

7. Walter de la Mare, "The Cupboard" in *Peacock Pie* (New York: Alfred A. Knopf, 1961), p. 26. Reprinted by permission of The Literary Trustees of Walter de la Mare, and The Society of Authors as their representative.

Experiencing Literature

While preschoolers can tolerate a surprising number of words they do not fully understand, there is a limit to their patience. It is best not to have too many words beyond their comprehension. A few new words are desirable, however, as exposure to new words helps children learn, increases their own word power, and identifies poetry as something a little out of the ordinary. Children will notice that unusual words often appear in poems they enjoy, and this knowledge will prepare them for adult poetry later.

For the most part, the subjects of poems for this age group should be related to the experiences and interests of children. These usually include animals, nature, playtime and toys, other children, grown-up people they meet, nonsense, and all kinds of transportation. Attention spans are short, so avoid long poems that are very involved and develop ideas beyond the comprehension of young children.

Adults need not be afraid to experiment, however, in choosing poetry for reading. The children, never reticent in letting their true feelings be known, may surprise the reader with their likes and dislikes and their ability to comprehend ideas. Selections should not be limited to poems with instant appeal; children respond to the quieter, mood poems as well.

How should poetry be read so that it will be loved and understood? Slowly, slowly, slowly. It is almost impossible to read too slowly. It takes time to create the mental pictures; it takes time to relate poetry to personal experience. A good poem offers a lot to think about. Each word is important and deserves full attention so the listener can appreciate all that the word conveys.

The reader should enter wholeheartedly into the emotional appeal of the poem. Once when a babysitter was reading aloud to a four-year-old, the child asked, "That was funny, wasn't it?" When the sitter answered, "Yes, it was funny," the child followed with, "Then why didn't you laugh?" Children want others to participate in their enjoyment, and they need outward, visible evidence that the reader shares their feelings. The adult, also, experiences greater enjoyment in reading aloud when feelings are expressed uninhibitedly.

Who should read poetry to children? Really, everyone who can read. The best place? The home is ideal. Parents can begin with lullabies. Older brothers and sisters who have loved certain poems in their early years are also good readers because their enthusiasm is sure to be contagious. "But," some may ask, "can they read with expression?" Perhaps they will. Older children will probably remember the way they heard the poem read to them and read in a similar manner. Fathers, too, with their wonderful range of pitch and their dramatic flair are naturals for poetry reading. Occasionally babysitters can be encouraged to share poetry along with the picture books that are at hand. Visiting relatives may also be invited to read poetry. People outside the immediate family may be surprised and pleased to learn how much little children enjoy this type of literature.

The same poems should be read over and over again. Children find great pleasure in hearing the familiar. Frequent repetition usually leads to effortless memorization, and lots of poetry is fun to repeat in unison "by heart."

It is important to have poetry available in the home so that family members and others may select poems to read to young children. Because poetry books are loved more the oftener they are read, it would be good to own some. Such volumes transcend age groups because a good poem is a good poem for everyone. To supplement the poetry books in the home, many good ones may be borrowed from the library. What's more, there are new ones each year! Sometimes whole books are compiled for the preschooler. Most books of poetry have sections for younger children, or at the very least, a number of suitable poems.

Good public library preschool story hours include carefully selected poetry. Some poems may be used very effectively with certain books. (A list at the end of this article gives specific suggestions.) The changing seasons and the weather offer ideal times for nature poems: the first snow, blustery winds, the coming of spring, a sudden thundershower, the initial appearance of dandelions.

A staff member of a nursery school or day care center can often get to know children well enough to relate specific poems to their personal experiences. Frequently in show-and-tell the children will talk about their pets, giving the adult in charge an opportunity to share "The Furry Ones" by Aileen Fisher:

I like
the furry ones
the waggy ones
the purry ones
the hoppy ones
that hurry,

The glossy ones
the saucy ones
the sleepy ones
the leapy ones
the mousy ones
that scurry,

The snuggly ones
the huggly ones
the never, never
ugly ones...
all soft
and warm
and furry [8]

Those who work with preschoolers have opportunities to help the children stretch their poetry appreciation beyond the jingle and rhyme levels. Choos-

---

8. Aileen Fisher, "The Furry Ones" in *Feathered Ones and Furry* (New York: Thomas Y. Crowell, 1971), p. viii. © 1971 by Aileen Fisher; by permission of Thomas Y. Crowell Company, Inc., publisher.

ing poetry with vivid imagery helps appreciation grow. "The Falling Star" by Sara Teasdale would be one good selection:

> I saw a star slide down the sky,
> Blinding the north as it went by,
> Too burning and too quick to hold,
> Too lovely to be bought or sold,
> Good only to make wishes on
> And then forever to be gone.[9]

Another suggestion for those who work with groups of children is to select a special poem for each day of the week. Repetition of that poem will make it very familiar and more understandable. Of course, readers may look for new poems—ones new to themselves as well as to the children. There is sometimes a tendency to think back on one's own childhood, remember all the traditional poetry, and thus miss the work of exciting new poets. Regular examination of new books of poetry and of current periodicals can help librarians and others avoid this pitfall.

Those working with preschoolers may experiment with having the children repeat certain poems or parts of poems in the manner of choral reading. As a beginning, the children could join the reader with the last line of each stanza or a repeated phrase. A poem that lends itself well to this sort of involvement is "Did You Feed My Cow?" from the book by the same title, compiled by Margaret Burroughs (Follett). Each stanza begins with a question and ends with a response. It is well to introduce this kind of interaction slowly and thoroughly so the children feel comfortable with the words when their turn comes.

Whatever poetry is shared with preschoolers, the adult should enjoy it thoroughly. There is nothing like enthusiasm to influence the children. If they see the grown-up really enjoying an experience, they will be quick to assume that attitude. Children deserve the opportunity to grow. Their taste and their ability to appreciate should never be underestimated. Appreciation for *anything* is difficult to teach; it usually has to be absorbed gradually. If a taste for poetry can be established early, the feeling of pleasure and an attitude of appreciation are likely to endure for years to come. Poetry *can* be picked to please preschoolers!

Poetry-Storytelling Bouquet

Poetry can add a new dimension to preschool story time. The following list suggests specific poems that relate to subject interests of preschoolers and

---

9. Sara Teasdale, "The Falling Star" in *Collected Poems* (New York: Macmillan Publishing Co., 1958), p. 198. Copyright 1930 by Sara Teasdale Filsinger, renewed 1958 by Guaranty Trust Company of New York, Executor.

includes picture book stories that can be shared with the poetry. (Complete bibliographic information is given in the section that follows. If the author of an individual poem is not given, the name is the same as that given for the collection.)

Babies

Poems
"Hiding" from *Everything and Anything* (Aldis)
"Little" (Aldis) from *Time for Poetry* (Arbuthnot)

Stories
A Baby Sitter for Frances (Hoban)
Peter's Chair (Keats)
The Bundle Book (Krauss)
Little Bear (Minarik)
The Box with Red Wheels (Petersham)

Bears

Poems
"Grizzly Bear" (Austin) from *Time for Poetry* (Arbuthnot)
"Furry Bear" (Milne) from *First Book of Poetry* (Peterson)
"The Black Bear" from *The Pack Rat's Day* (Prelutsky)

Stories
"The Three Bears" from *The Golden Goose Book* (Brooke)
Beady Bear (Freeman)
Blueberries for Sal (McCloskey)
I'm Going on a Bear Hunt (Sivulich)

Bedtime

Poems
"A Sleepy Song" (Bacon) from *Ring-a-Round* (Harrington)
"Bedtime" from *In One Door and out the Other* (Fisher)
"Good Night" from *In One Door and out the Other* (Fisher)
"Not Tonight" from *Is Somewhere Always Far Away?* (Jacobs)
"Crescent Moon" (Roberts) from *Time for Poetry* (Arbuthnot)

Stories
Lisa Cannot Sleep (Beckman)
Goodnight Moon (Brown)
Bedtime for Frances (Hoban)
All the Pretty Horses (Jeffers)
Edie Changes Her Mind (Johnston)
Milton the Early Riser (Kraus)

Experiencing Literature

The Moon Jumpers (Udry)
The Summer Night (Zolotow)

Birthdays

Poems
"Birthday" from *In One Door and out the Other* (Fisher)
"The Miracle" (Fowler) from *Birthday Candles Burning Bright* (Brewton)
"The Birthday Child" (Fyleman) from *Poetry for Holidays* (Larrick)
"A Party" from *Tirra Lirra* (Richards)
Stories
The Secret Birthday Message (Carle)
Ask Mr. Bear (Flack)
Lyle and the Birthday Party (Waber)
Margaret's Birthday (Wahl)
Mr. Rabbit and the Lovely Present (Zolotow)

Boats

Poems
"Boats" (Bennett) from *Time for Poetry* (Arbuthnot)
"My Little Boat" from *Ring-a-Round* (Harrington)
"The Bridge" from *Is Somewhere Always Far Away?* (Jacobs)
"The Bridge" from *Sing-Song* (Rossetti)
"Where Go the Boats" from *A Child's Garden of Verses* (Stevenson)
"Ferry-Boats" (Tippett) from *Time for Poetry* (Arbuthnot)
Stories
Little Toot (Gramatky)
The Little Red Lighthouse and the Great Gray Bridge (Swift)
Skiddycock Pond (Tudor)

Books and Libraries

Poems
"The Fairy Book" (Brown) from *My Poetry Book* (Huffard)
"Reading" from *Rhymes about Us* (Chute)
"Choosing" (Farjeon) from *Time for Poetry* (Arbuthnot)
"My Book Holds Many Stories" (Wynne) from *Highdays and Holidays* (Adams)
Stories
Petunia (Duvoisin)
Rosa-Too-Little (Felt)
Quiet—There's a Canary in the Library (Freeman)
1, 2, 3 for the Library (Little)
Mike's House (Sauer)

Cats

Poems
"The Little Kittens" (Follen) from *Time for Poetry* (Arbuthnot)
"Cat" (Miller) from *Time for Poetry* (Arbuthnot)
"Pussy Cat, Pussy Cat" (Mother Goose) from *Time for Poetry* (Arbuthnot)
"Our Pussy Cat" (North) from *From Little to Big* (Vance)
"The Cats of Kilkenny" from *The Golden Treasury of Poetry* (Untermeyer)
Stories
Green Eyes (Birnbaum)
Millions of Cats (Gag)
Three Kittens (Ginsburg)
The So-So Cat (Hurd)
The Fat Cat (Kent)
Find the Cat (Livermore)
Rich Cat, Poor Cat (Waber)
The Tale of a Black Cat (Withers)

Chickens

Poems
"The Mouse, the Frog and the Little Red Hen" (Anonymous) from *The Barnes Book of Nursery Verse* (Ireson)
"The Chickens" (Fyleman) from *Time for Poetry* (Arbuthnot)
"The Hens" (Roberts) from *The Golden Treasury of Poetry* (Untermeyer)
"Red Hen" from *Crickety-Cricket!* (Tippett)
Stories
Little Hatchy Hen (Flora)
Henny Penny and Chicken Little (Galdone)
The Little Red Hen (Galdone)
The Chick and the Duckling (Ginsburg)
Rosie's Walk (Hutchins)
Chicken Licken (McLeish)

Christmas

Poems
"Christmas Stocking" (Farjeon) from *Poetry for the Holidays* (Larrick)
"At Christmas Time" from *In One Door and out the Other* (Fisher)
"Christmas Mouse" (Fisher) from *Poetry for the Holidays* (Larrick)
"Christmas Tree" from *In One Door and out the Other* (Fisher)
"Winter" from *In One Door and out the Other* (Fisher)
"A City Street at Christmas" from *Crickety-Cricket!* (Tippett)
"Counting the Days" from *Crickety-Cricket!* (Tippett)
"My Christmas Tree" from *Crickety-Cricket!* (Tippett)

Experiencing Literature

My Slippers Are Red (Steiner)
Mr. Rabbit and the Lovely Present (Zolotow)

Crocodiles

Poems
"If You Should Meet a Crocodile" (Author unknown) from *From Little to Big* (Vance)
"How Doth the Little Crocodile" (Carroll) from *Time for Poetry* (Arbuthnot)
"The Monkeys and the Crocodile" (Richards) from *Time for Poetry* (Arbuthnot)
"The Crocodile's Toothache" from *Where the Sidewalk Ends* (Silverstein)
Stories
Keep Your Mouth Closed, Dear (Aliki)
Crocodile's Tale (Aruego)
Crocodile and Hen (Lexau)
The House on East 88th Street (Waber)
Lovable Lyle (Waber)
Lyle, Lyle Crocodile (Waber)

Dogs

Poems
"I Like Dogs" (Brown) from *From Little to Big* (Vance)
"My Dog" (Chute) from *First Book of Poetry* (Peterson)
"My Dog Ginger" from *In One Door and out the Other* (Fisher)
"My Puppy" (Fisher) from *Round about Six* (Rawlins)
"Puppy and I" (Milne) from *Time for Poetry* (Arbuthnot)
Stories
Clifford, the Big Red Dog (Bridwell)
Lengthy (Holl)
Whistle for Willie (Keats)
All the Lassies (Skorpen)
Harry, the Dirty Dog (Zion)

Dragons

Poems
"The Dragon with a Big Nose" (Henderson) from *Round about Six* (Rawlins)
"The Tale of Custard the Dragon" (Nash) from *The Big Golden Book of Poetry* (Werner)
Stories
The Dragon in the Clock Box (Craig)
The Dragon Takes a Wife (Myers)
The Dragon Who Liked to Spit Fire (Varga)

Experiencing Literature

Ducks

Poems

"Quack!" (de la Mare) from *Time for Poetry* (Arbuthnot)
"The Ducklings" from *Cricket in a Thicket* (Fisher)
"Ducks at Dawn" (Tippett) from *Time for Poetry* (Arbuthnot)

Stories

Angus and the Ducks (Flack)
Story about Ping (Flack)
Seven Diving Ducks (Friskey)
Hamilton Duck (Getz)
Hamilton Duck's Springtime Story (Getz)
Make Way for Ducklings (McCloskey)

Easter

Poems

"Meeting the Easter Bunny" (Bennett) from *Sung under the Silver Umbrella* (Assn. for Childhood Ed.)
"Jelly Beans" from *In One Door and out the Other* (Fisher)
"Easter Morning—Poems 1 and 2" from *Away and Ago* (McCord)

Stories

The Humbug Rabbit (Balian)
The Golden Egg Book (Brown)
The Easter Bunny That Overslept (Friedrich)
The Country Bunny and the Little Gold Shoes (Heyward)
The Bunny Who Found Easter (Zolotow)

Elephants

Poems

"I Asked My Mother" (Anonymous) from *The Moon Is Shining Bright as Day* (Nash)
"Elephant" (Asquith) from *Sung under the Silver Umbrella* (Assn. for Childhood Ed.)
"The Elephant" (Belloc) from *Round about Six* (Rawlins)
"Holding Hands" (Link) from *From Little to Big* (Vance)
"Eletelephony" from *Tirra Lirra* (Richards)

Stories

Story of Babar (Brunhoff)
Horton Hatches the Egg (Seuss)
The Elephant and the Bad Baby (Vipont)

Foxes

Poems

"As Soon as It's Fall" from *Cricket in a Thicket* (Fisher)
"Night of Wing" (Frost) from *Time for Poetry* (Arbuthnot)
"The Fox and the Chickens" (Morgenstern) from *The Fox Book* (Shaw)
"Sly Is the Word" from *The Fox Book* (Shaw)

Stories

One Fine Day (Hogrogian)
The Tomten and the Fox (Lindgren)
The Fox Went Out on a Chilly Night (Spier)

Friends

Poems

"Jonathan Bing" (Brown) from *The First Book of Poetry* (Peterson)
"New Neighbors" from *In One Door and out the Other* (Fisher)
"Susan Blue" (Greenaway) from *My Poetry Book* (Huffard)
"The Invisible Playmate" (Widdemer) from *My Poetry Book* (Huffard)

Stories

A Friend Is Someone Who Likes You (Anglund)
Do You Want to Be My Friend? (Carle)
May I Bring a Friend? (De Regniers)
Play with Me (Ets)
My Friend John (Zolotow)

Frogs

Poems

"Grandfather Frog" (Bechtel) from *Time for Poetry* (Arbuthnot)
"Twenty Froggies" (Cooper) from *The Frog Book* (Shaw)
"The Frog and I" from *In One Door and out the Other* (Fisher)
"Green Frog" from *Crickety Cricket!* (Tippett)

Stories

Frog Went a-Courtin' (Langstaff)
Frog and Toad Are Friends (Lobel)
Walter Was a Frog (Massie)

Giants and Elves

Poems

"The Little Elfman" (Bangs) from *Time for Poetry* (Arbuthnot)
"Momotara" (Fyleman) from *Time for Poetry* (Arbuthnot)
"The Greedy Giant" from *Tirra Lirra* (Richards)

Stories

Jim and the Beanstalk (Briggs)

*The History of Mother Twaddle and the Marvelous Achievements of Her Son
    Jack* (Galdone)
Giant John (Lobel)
The Little Giant Girl and the Elf Boy (Minarik)

Halloween

Poems
"What Am I?" (Aldis) from *Poetry for Holidays* (Larrick)
"Halloween" (Behn) from *Time for Poetry* (Arbuthnot)
"The Goblin" (Fyleman) from *Time for Poetry* (Arbuthnot)
"What Witches Do" from *Is Somewhere Always Far Away?* (Jacobs)
"Black and Gold" (Turner) from *Time for Poetry* (Arbuthnot)
Stories
A Woggle of Witches (Adams)
The Humbug Witch (Balian)
Clifford's Halloween (Bridwell)
Georgie (Bright)
Space Witch (Freeman)
One Dark Night (Preston)
Scat, the Witch's Cat (Ross)
The Kitten in the Pumpkin Patch (Shaw)
Trick or Treat (Slobodkin)
Gus Was a Friendly Ghost (Woolley)
A Tiger Called Thomas (Zolotow)

Hats

Poems
"The Little Hat" from *All Together* (Aldis)
Stories
Jennie's Hat (Keats)
Who Took the Farmer's Hat? (Nodset)
The 500 Hats of Bartholomew Cubbins (Seuss)

Houses

Poems
"Two Cozy Homes" from *Listen! and Help Tell the Story* (Carlson)
"The Cupboard" (de la Mare) from *Bridled with Rainbows* (Brewton)
"Some One" (de la Mare) from *Time for Poetry* (Arbuthnot)
"The Shiny Little House" (Hayes) from *Sung under the Silver Umbrella* (Assn.
    for Childhood Ed.)
"The Butterbean Tent" (Roberts) from *Sung under the Silver Umbrella* (Assn.
    for Childhood Ed.)

"Tree House" from *Where the Sidewalk Ends* (Silverstein)
Stories
The Little House (Burton)
The House That Jack Built (Galdone)
You Ought to See Herbert's House (Lund)
Always Room for One More (Leodhas)

Imaginary Animals

Poems
"The Spangled Pandemonium" (Brown) from *Time for Poetry* (Arbuthnot)
"After a Visit to the Natural History Museum" from *Tirra Lirra* (Richards)
"My Griffin" from *Tirra Lirra* (Richards)
Stories
The Aminal (Balian)
The Funny Thing (Gag)
A Lion in the Meadow (Mahy)
Sam, Bangs, and Moonshine (Ness)
The Alligator under the Bed (Nixon)

Lions

Poems
"Why Nobody Pets the Lion at the Zoo" (Ciardi) from *From Little to Big* (Vance)
"The Lion" from *The Pack Rat's Day* (Prelutsky)
"The Lion and the Fox" (Rees) from *Time for Poetry* (Arbuthnot)
"Lions Running over the Green" (Wynne) from *Under the Tent of the Sky* (Brewton)
Stories
Andy and the Lion (Daugherty)
The Happy Lion (Fatio)
Dandelion (Freeman)
The Lion and the Rat (La Fontaine)

Mice

Poems
"The Mouse" (Coatsworth) from *Time for Poetry* (Arbuthnot)
"Mice" (Fyleman) from *Time for Poetry* (Arbuthnot)
"The House of the Mouse" (Mitchell) from *Time for Poetry* (Arbuthnot)
"The House Mouse" from *The Pack Rat's Day* (Prelutsky)
"The Pack Rat" from *The Pack Rat's Day* (Prelutsky)
"The City Mouse" (Rossetti) from *Sung under the Silver Umbrella* (Assn. for Childhood Ed.)

Experiencing Literature

Stories
Once a Mouse (Hitopadesa)
Whose Mouse Are You? (Kraus)
Alexander and the Wind-Up Mouse (Lionni)
Frederick (Lionni)
Mousekin's Golden House (Miller)
Henry the Uncatchable Mouse (Simon)
Amos and Boris (Steig)
Anatole (Titus)

Monkeys

Poems
"So Many Monkeys" (Edey) from *Time for Poetry* (Arbuthnot)
"The Monkeys and the Crocodile" (Richards) from *Time for Poetry*
    (Arbuthnot)
"The Monkeys" (Thompson) from *Time for Poetry* (Arbuthnot)
Stories
Curious George (Rey)
Caps for Sale (Slobodkina)
Cool Ride in the Sky (Wolkestein)

Monsters

Poems
"The Goblin" (Fyleman) from *Time for Poetry* (Arbuthnot)
"A Goblinade" (Jacques) from *Time for Poetry* (Arbuthnot)
"Wild Beasts" (Stein) from *Under the Tent of the Sky* (Brewton)
Stories
The Something (Babbitt)
Goodnight Orange Monster (Lifton)
There's a Nightmare in My Closet (Mayer)
Where the Wild Things Are (Sendak)
My Mama Says There Aren't Any Zombies, Ghosts, Vampires, Creatures,
    Demons, Monsters, Fiends, Goblins or Things (Viorst)

Naughty Children

Poems
"Bad" from *Here, There, and Everywhere* (Aldis)
"Good-Bye Impey" from *Listen! and Help Tell the Story* (Carlson)
"Music Box" from *In One Door and out the Other* (Fisher)
"So Still" from *In One Door and out the Other* (Fisher)
"The Story of Augustus" (Hoffman) from *Time for Poetry* (Arbuthnot)
"Punishment" from *Catch Me a Wind* (Hubbell)

"How Quiet?" from *Is Somewhere Always Far Away?* (Jacobs)
"The Good Little Girl" (Milne) from *Beastly Boys and Ghastly Girls* (Cole)
"Sometimes" from *Catch a Little Rhyme* (Merriam)
"Pleasant Street" from *Woody and Me* (Neville)
"Wild Beasts" (Stein) from *Under the Tent of the Sky* (Brewton)
Stories
The Judge (Zemach)
The Little Brute Family (Hoban)
Prince Bertram the Bad (Lobel)
Pierre (Sendak)
Where the Wild Things Are (Sendak)
Alexander and the Terrible, Horrible, No Good, Very Bad Day (Viorst)

Numbers

Poems
"Head and Shoulders, Baby" from *Did You Feed My Cow?* (Burroughs)
One, Two, Buckle My Shoe; a Book of Counting Rhymes (Illustrated by Gail E. Haley)
Stories
The Very Hungry Caterpillar (Carle)
Chicken Little, Count to Ten (Friskey)
Over in the Meadow (Langstaff)
10 Bears in My Bed (Mack)
Numbers (Reiss)
Jeanne Marie Counts Her Sheep (Seignobosc)
One Was Johnny (Sendak)

Pigs

Poems
"The Old Woman and the Pig" from *Did You Feed My Cow?* (Burroughs)
"Mary Middling" (Fyleman) from *Sung under the Silver Umbrella* (Assn. for Childhood Ed.)
"Sizes" from *From Little to Big* (Vance)
Stories
"The Three Little Pigs," from *The Golden Goose Book* (Brooke)
The Old Woman and Her Pig (Galdone)
Yummers! (Marshall)
The Piggy in the Puddle (Pomerantz)

Rabbits

Poems
"Rabbits" (Baruch) from *Sung under the Silver Umbrella* (Assn. for Childhood Ed.)

"The Rabbit and the Fox" (Sansom) from *Round about Six* (Rawlins)
"The Rabbit" (Roberts) from *The Golden Treasury of Poetry* (Untermeyer)
"Mr. Rabbit" (Willson) from *From Little to Big* (Vance)
Stories
The Runaway Bunny (Brown)
Where's the Bunny? (Carroll)
Tale of Peter Rabbit (Potter)
Mr. Rabbit and the Lovely Present (Zolotow)

Rain

Poems
"The Rain" from *Everything and Anything* (Aldis)
"The Reason" (Aldis) from *Time for Poetry* (Arbuthnot)
"Showers" from *Rhymes about Us* (Chute)
"The Elf and the Dormouse" (Herford) from *The First Book of Poetry*
    (Peterson)
"April Rain Song" from *Don't You Turn Back* (Hughes)
"Rain Song" from *Is Somewhere Always Far Away?* (Jacobs)
"Weather" from *Catch a Little Rhyme* (Merriam)
"Umbrella Brigade" (Richards) from *Sung under the Silver Umbrella* (Assn.
    for Childhood Ed.)
"Little Rain" (Roberts) from *Time for Poetry* (Arbuthnot)
"Rain" from *A Child's Garden of Verses* (Stevenson)
"Play After Rain" from *Crickety-Cricket!* (Tippett)
Stories
Pete's Puddle (Foster)
Mushroom in the Rain (Ginsburg)
Rain Makes Applesauce (Scheer)
Umbrella (Yashima)

School

Poems
"September" from *In One Door and out the Other* (Fisher)
"Mary Had a Little Lamb" from *Mother Goose*
"Higgledy Piggledy" from *Tirra Lirra* (Richards)
Stories
Shawn Goes to School (Breinburg)
Pocketful of Cricket (Caudill)
New Teacher (Cohen)
Will I Have a Friend? (Cohen)
Crictor (Ungerer)

Shoes

Poems

"The Cobbler" (Chaffee) from *Time for Poetry* (Arbuthnot)
"An Event" from *Rhymes about Us* (Chute)
"Shoe Laces" from *Is Somewhere Always Far Away?* (Jacobs)
"Shoes" (Robinson) from *Time for Poetry* (Arbuthnot)
"New Shoes" (Wilkins) from *Sung under the Silver Umbrella* (Assn. for
  Childhood Ed.)
"Choosing Shoes" (Wolfe) from *Sung under the Silver Umbrella* (Assn. for
  Childhood Ed.)

Stories

Down, Down the Mountain (Credle)
What Can You Do with a Shoe? (De Regniers)
Fit for a King (Sheldon)

Snow

Poems

"Winter Night" from *Rhymes about Us* (Chute)
"White Morning" from *In One Door and out the Other* (Fisher)
"Winter Day" from *In One Door and out the Other* (Fisher)
"Winter Walk" from *In One Door and out the Other* (Fisher)
"Why Does It Snow?" (Richards) from *Bridled with Rainbows* (Brewton)
"White Fields" (Stephens) from *Round about Six* (Rawlins)
"Tracks in Snow" from *Crickety-Cricket!* (Tippett)
"Snow" (Wilkins) from *Time for Poetry* (Arbuthnot)

Stories

Katy and the Big Snow (Burton)
The Snowy Day (Keats)
The Tomten (Lindgren)
White Snow, Bright Snow (Tressell)

Teddy Bears

Poems

"Teddy Bear" (Behn) from *Time for Poetry* (Arbuthnot)
"My Teddy Bear" from *Rhymes about Us* (Chute)
"Us Two" from *Now We Are Six* (Milne)
"My Teddy Bear" (Olgin) from *Away We Go* (McEwen)

Stories

Alfred Goes House Hunting (Binzen)
Corduroy (Freeman)
Arthur's Honey Bear (Hoban)
Ira Sleeps Over (Waber)

Experiencing Literature

Trains

Poems

"A Modern Dragon" (Bennett) from *Under the Tent of the Sky* (Brewton)
"The Baby Goes to Boston" (Richards) from *Time for Poetry* (Arbuthnot)
"The Engine Driver" (Sansom) from *Round about Six* (Rawlins)
"Trains" (Tippett) from *Time for Poetry* (Arbuthnot)
"The Song of the Engine" (Worsley-Benison) from *Round about Six* (Rawlins)

Stories

Choo, Choo (Burton)
Little Engine That Could (Piper)

Trees

Poems

"Trees" (Behn) from *Time for Poetry* (Arbuthnot)
"Best of All" from *Cricket in a Thicket* (Fisher)
"Climbing" (Fisher) from *Time for Poetry* (Arbuthnot)
"Every Time I Climb a Tree" from *Every Time I Climb a Tree* (McCord)
"The Swing" from *Child's Garden of Verses* (Stevenson)
"The Tree Stands Very Straight and Still" (Wynne) from *Sung under the Silver Umbrella* (Assn. for Childhood Ed.)

Stories

The Paper Flower Tree (Ayer)
The Giving Tree (Silverstein)
A Tree Is Nice (Udry)

Turtles

Poems

"A Discovery" (Knipe) from *Feather or Fur* (Mannheim)
"The Little Turtle" (Lindsay) from *Sung under the Silver Umbrella* (Assn. for Childhood Ed.)
"Turtle" from *Crickety-Cricket!* (Tippett)

Stories

Timothy Turtle (Davis)
Theodore Turtle (MacGregor)
The Tortoise's Tug of War (Maestro)
Yertle the Turtle (Seuss)

Vegetables

Poems

"If I Were My Mother" from *In One Door and out the Other* (Fisher)
"Seeds" from *Cricket in a Thicket* (Fisher)
"Peculiar" from *Catch a Little Rhyme* (Merriam)

"Growing in the Vale" (Rossetti) from *Ring-A-Round* (Harrington)
"Vegetables" (Silverstein) from *Oh, That's Ridiculous* (Cole)
"Company" from *Crickety-Cricket!* (Tippett)
Stories
Carrot Seed (Kraus)
Blue Bug's Vegetable Garden (Poulet)
The Great Big Enormous Turnip (Tolstoy)

Wind

Poems
"A Kite" (Author unknown) from *Time for Poetry* (Arbuthnot)
"Who Has Seen the Wind?" (Rossetti) from *The First Book of Poetry* (Peterson)
"The Wind" from *Child's Garden of Verses* (Stevenson)
"Windy Weather" from *Crickety-Cricket!* (Tippett)
Stories
Gilberto and the Wind (Ets)
The Wind Blew (Hutchins)
The North Wind and the Sun (La Fontaine)
Curious George Flies a Kite (Rey)
The March Wind (Rice)

Zoo

Poems
"Inside the Zoo" from *Catch a Little Rhyme* (Merriam)
"Excuse Us, Animals in the Zoo" (Wynne) from *Under the Tent of the Sky* (Brewton)
Stories
1, 2, 3 to the Zoo (Carle)
Be Nice to Spiders (Graham)
A Zoo for Mr. Muster (Lobel)
Zoo, Where Are You? (McGovern)
The Zoo That Moved (Miklowitz)
Bruno Munari's Zoo (Munari)

Picture Books Cited

Adams, Adrienne. *A Woggle of Witches.* Illus. by the author. New York: Charles Scribner's Sons, 1971.
Aliki. *Keep Your Mouth Closed, Dear.* Illus. by the author. New York: Dial Press, 1966.
Anglund, Joan Walsh. *A Friend Is Someone Who Likes You.* Illus. by the author. New York: Harcourt Brace Jovanovich, Inc., 1958.

Experiencing Literature

Aruego, Jose. *A Crocodile's Tale.* Illus. by the author. New York: Charles Scribner's Sons, 1972.

Ayer, Jacqueline. *The Paper-Flower Tree.* Illus. by the author. New York: Harcourt Brace Jovanovich, Inc., 1962.

Babbitt, Natalie. *The Something.* Illus. by the author. New York: Farrar, Straus & Giroux, Inc., 1970.

Balian, Lorna. *The Aminal.* Illus. by the author. Nashville: Abingdon Press, 1972.

———. *The Humbug Rabbit.* Illus. by the author. Nashville: Abingdon Press, 1974.

———. *The Humbug Witch.* Illus. by the author. Nashville: Abingdon Press, 1965.

Barrett, Judith. *Animals Should Definitely Not Wear Clothing.* Illus. by Ron Barrett. New York: Atheneum Publishers, 1970.

Beckman, Kaj. *Lisa Cannot Sleep.* Illus. by Per Beckman. New York: Franklin Watts, Inc., 1969.

Beskow, Elsa. *Pelle's New Suit.* Illus. by the author. New York: Harper & Row, Publishers, Inc., 1929.

Binzen, Bill. *Alfred Goes House Hunting.* Illus. by the author. New York: Doubleday Publishing Co., 1974.

Birnbaum, Abe. *Green Eyes.* Illus. by the author. New York: Capitol Publishing Co., 1953.

Breinburg, Petronella. *Shawn Goes to School.* Illus. by Errol Lloyd. New York: Thomas Y. Crowell Company, Inc., 1974.

Bridwell, Norman. *Clifford the Big Red Dog.* Illus. by the author. New York: Scholastic Book Service, 1966.

———. *Clifford's Halloween.* Illus. by the author. New York: Scholastic Book Service, 1967.

Briggs, Raymond. *Jim and the Beanstalk.* Illus. by the author. New York: Coward-McCann & Geoghegan, Inc., 1970.

Bright, Robert. *Georgie.* Illus. by the author. New York: Doubleday Publishing Co., 1959.

Brooke, L. Leslie. "The Three Bears" from *The Golden Goose Book.* Illus. by the compiler. New York: Frederick Warne & Co., 1905.

Brown, Marcia. *Once a Mouse.* Illus. by the author. New York: Charles Scribner's Sons, 1961.

Brown, Margaret Wise. *The Golden Egg Book.* Illus. by Clement Hurd. New York: Harper & Row Publishers, Inc., 1947.

———. *Goodnight Moon.* Illus. by Clement Hurd. New York: Harper & Row Publishers, Inc., 1947.

———. *The Runaway Bunny.* Illus. by Clement Hurd. New York: Harper & Row Publishers, Inc., 1972.

Brunhoff, Jean de. *Story of Babar.* Illus. by the author. New York: Random House, Inc., 1937.

Burton, Virginia. *Choo, Choo.* Illus. by the author. Boston: Houghton Mifflin Co., 1937.

———. *Katy and the Big Snow.* Illus. by the author. Boston: Houghton Mifflin Co., 1943.

———. *The Little House.* Illus. by the author. Boston: Houghton Mifflin Co., 1942.

Carle, Eric. *Do You Want to Be My Friend?* Illus. by the author. New York: Thomas Y. Crowell Company, Inc., 1971.

———. *1, 2, 3 to the Zoo.* Illus. by the author. Cleveland: Collins-World Publishing Co., Inc., 1968.

———. *The Secret Birthday Message.* Illus. by the author. New York: Thomas Y. Crowell Company, Inc., 1972.

———. *The Very Hungry Caterpillar.* Illus. by the author. Cleveland: Collins-World Publishing Co., Inc., 1970.

Carroll, Ruth. *Where's the Bunny?* Illus. by the author. New York: Henry Z. Walck, Inc., 1950.

Caudill, Rebecca. *A Pocketful of Cricket.* Illus. by Evaline Ness. New York: Holt, Rinehart & Winston, Inc., 1964.

Cohen, Miriam. *The New Teacher.* Illus. by Lillian Hoban. New York: Macmillan Publishing Co., Inc., 1974.

———. *Will I Have a Friend?* Illus. by Lillian Hoban. New York: Macmillan Publishing Co., Inc., 1967.

Craig, M. Jean. *The Dragon in the Clock Box.* Illus. by Kelly Oechsli. New York: W. W. Norton & Co., Inc., 1962.

Credle, Ellis. *Down, Down the Mountain.* Illus. by the author. Camden, N.J.: Thomas Nelson, Inc., 1934.

Daugherty, James. *Andy and the Lion.* Illus. by the author. New York: Viking Press, Inc., 1938.

Davis, Alice V. *Timothy Turtle.* Illus. by Guy B. Wiser. New York: Harcourt Brace Jovanovich, Inc., 1940.

De Paola, Tomie. *Charlie Needs a Cloak.* Illus. by the author. Englewood Cliffs, N.J.: Prentice-Hall, Inc., 1974.

De Regniers, Beatrice. *Circus.* Illus. by Al Giese. New York: Viking Press, Inc., 1966.

———. *May I Bring a Friend?* Illus. by Beni Montresor. New York: Atheneum Publishers, 1964.

———. *What Can You Do with a Shoe?* Illus. by Maurice Sendak. New York: Harper & Row Publishers, Inc., 1955.

Duvoisin, Roger. *Petunia.* Illus. by the author. New York: Alfred A. Knopf, Inc., 1950.

Ets, Marie Hall. *Gilberto and the Wind.* Illus. by the author. New York: Viking Press, Inc., 1963.

————. *Play with Me.* Illus. by the author. New York: Viking Press, Inc., 1955.

Fatio, Louise. *The Happy Lion.* Illus. by Roger Duvoisin. New York: McGraw-Hill Book Co., 1954.

Felt, Sue. *Rosa-Too-Little.* Illus. by the author. New York: Doubleday Publishing Co., 1950.

Fenton, Edward. *Big Yellow Balloon.* Illus. by Ib Ohlsson. New York: Doubleday Publishing Co., 1967.

Flack, Marjorie. *Angus and the Ducks.* Illus. by the author. New York: Doubleday Publishing Co., 1939.

————. *Ask Mr. Bear.* Illus. by the author. New York: Macmillan Publishing Co., Inc., 1932.

————. *Story about Ping.* Illus. by Kurt Wiese. New York: Viking Press, Inc., 1933.

Flora, James. *Little Hatchy Hen.* Illus. by the author. New York: Harcourt Brace Jovanovich, Inc., 1969.

Foster, Joanna. *Pete's Puddle.* Illus. by Beatrice Darwin. New York: Harcourt Brace Jovanovich, Inc., 1969.

Freeman, Don. *Beady Bear.* Illus. by the author. New York: Viking Press, Inc., 1954.

————. *Corduroy.* Illus. by the author. New York: Viking Press, Inc., 1968.

————. *Dandelion.* Illus. by the author. New York: Viking Press, Inc., 1965.

————. *Quiet! There's a Canary in the Library.* Illus. by the author. San Carlos, Calif.: Golden Gate Junior Books, 1969.

————. *Space Witch.* Illus. by the author. New York: Viking Press, Inc., 1959.

Friedrich, Priscilla. *The Easter Bunny That Overslept.* Illus. by Adrienne Adams. New York: Lothrop, Lee & Shepard Co., 1957.

Friskey, Margaret. *Chicken Little, Count-to-Ten.* Illus. by K. Evans. Chicago: Children's Press, Inc., 1946.

————. *Seven Diving Ducks.* Illus. by Jean Morey. Chicago: Children's Press, Inc., 1965.

Gackenbach, Dick. *Claude the Dog.* Illus. by the author. New York: Seabury Press, Inc., 1974.

Gag, Wanda. *The Funny Thing.* Illus. by the author. New York: Coward, McCann & Geoghegan, Inc., 1929.

————. *Millions of Cats.* Illus. by the author. Eau Claire, Wis.: E. M. Hale & Company, 1928.

Galdone, Paul, Illus. *The History of Mother Twaddle and the Marvelous Achievements of Her Son Jack.* New York: Seabury Press, Inc., 1974.

————. *Henny Penny and Chicken Little.* New York: Seabury Press, Inc., 1968.

———. *The House That Jack Built.* New York: Seabury Press, Inc., 1961.

———. *The Little Red Hen.* New York: Seabury Press, Inc., 1973.

———. *The Old Woman and Her Pig.* New York: McGraw-Hill Book Co., 1961.

Getz, Arthur. *Hamilton Duck.* Illus. by the author. Racine: Western Publishing Co., Inc., 1972.

———. *Hamilton Duck's Springtime Story.* Illus. by the author. Racine: Western Publishing Co., Inc., 1974.

Ginsburg, Mirra. *The Chick and the Duckling.* Illus. by Jose and Ariane Aruego. New York: Macmillan Publishing Co., Inc., 1972.

———. *Mushroom in the Rain.* Illus. by Jose and Ariane Aruego. New York: Macmillan Publishing Co., Inc., 1974.

———. *Three Kittens.* Illus. by Giulio Maestro. New York: Crown Publishers, Inc., 1973.

Graham, Margaret. *Be Nice to Spiders.* Illus. by the author. Eau Claire, Wis.: E. M. Hale & Company, 1967.

Gramatky, Hardie. *Little Toot.* Illus. by the author. New York: G. P. Putnam's Sons, 1939.

Heyward, Dubose. *The Country Bunny and the Little Gold Shoes.* Illus. by Marjorie Flack. Boston: Houghton Mifflin Co., 1939.

Hoban, Lillian. *Arthur's Honey Bear.* Illus. by the author. New York: Harper & Row Publishers, Inc., 1974.

Hoban, Russell. *A Baby Sister for Frances.* Illus. by Lillian Hoban. New York: Harper & Row Publishers, Inc., 1964.

———. *Bedtime for Frances.* Illus. by Garth Williams. New York: Harper & Row Publishers, Inc., 1960.

———. *The Little Brute Family.* Illus. by Lillian Hoban. New York: Macmillan Publishing Co., Inc., 1966.

Hoff, Syd. *Lengthy.* Illus. by the author. New York: G. P. Putnam's Sons, 1964.

———. *Where's Prancer?* Illus. by the author. New York: Harper & Row Publishers, Inc., 1960.

Hogrogian, Nonny. *One Fine Day.* Illus. by the author. New York: Macmillan Publishing Co., Inc., 1971.

Hurd, Edith. *The So-So Cat.* Illus. by Clement Hurd. New York: Harper & Row Publishers, Inc., 1964.

Hutchins, Pat. *Rosie's Walk.* Illus. by the author. New York: Macmillan Publishing Co., Inc., 1968.

———. *The Silver Christmas Tree.* Illus. by the author. New York: Macmillan Publishing Co., Inc., 1974.

———. *The Wind Blew.* Illus. by the author. New York: Macmillan Publishing Co., Inc., 1974.

Jeffers, Susan. *All the Pretty Horses.* Illus. by the author. New York: Macmillan Publishing Co., Inc., 1974.

Johnston, Johanna. *Edie Changes Her Mind.* Illus. by Paul Galdone. New York: G. P. Putnam's Sons, 1964.

Keats, Ezra Jack. *Jennie's Hat.* Illus. by the author. New York: Harper & Row Publishers, Inc., 1966.

———. *Peter's Chair.* Illus. by the author. New York: Harper & Row Publishers, Inc., 1967.

———. *The Snowy Day.* Illus. by the author. New York: Viking Press, Inc., 1962.

———. *Whistle for Willie.* Illus. by the author. New York: Viking Press, Inc., 1964.

Kent, Jack. *The Fat Cat.* Illus. by the author. New York: Parents' Magazine Press, 1971.

Kraus, Robert. *Milton the Early Riser.* Illus. by Jose and Ariane Aruego. New York: Windmill Books, Inc., 1972.

———. *Whose Mouse Are You?* Illus. by Jose Aruego. New York: Macmillan Publishing Co., Inc., 1970.

Krauss, Ruth. *The Bundle Book.* Illus. by Helen Stone. New York: Harper & Row Publishers, Inc., 1951.

———. *The Carrot Seed.* Illus. by Crockett Johnson. New York: Harper & Row Publishers, Inc., 1945.

La Fontaine, Jean de. *The Lion and the Rat.* Illus. by Brian Wildsmith. New York: Franklin Watts, Inc., 1963.

———. *The North Wind and the Sun.* Illus. by Brian Wildsmith. New York: Franklin Watts, Inc., 1964.

Langstaff, John. *Frog Went a-Courtin'.* Illus. by Feodor Rojankovsky. New York: Harcourt Brace Jovanovich, Inc., 1955.

———. *Over in the Meadow.* Illus. by Feodor Rojankovsky. New York: Harcourt Brace Jovanovich, Inc., 1967.

Leodhas, Sorche Nic. *Always Room for One More.* Illus. by Nonny Hogrogian. New York: Holt, Rinehart & Winston, Inc., 1965.

Lexau, Joan. *Crocodile and Hen.* Illus. by Joan Sandin. New York: Harper & Row Publishers, Inc., 1969.

Lifton, Betty Jean. *Goodnight Orange Monster.* Illus. by Cyndy Szekeres. New York: Atheneum Publishers, 1972.

Lindgren, Astrid. *The Tomten.* Illus. by H. Wiberg. New York: Coward, McCann & Geoghegan, Inc., 1961.

———. *The Tomten and the Fox.* Illus. by H. Wiberg. New York: Coward, McCann & Geoghegan, Inc., 1965.

Lionni, Leo. *Alexander and the Wind-Up Mouse.* Illus. by the author. New York: Pantheon Books, 1969.

———. *Frederick.* Illus. by the author. New York: Pantheon Books, 1966.

———. *Little Blue and Little Yellow.* Illus. by the author. Stamford, Conn.: Astor-Honor, Inc., 1959.

Lipkind, William. *The Christmas Bunny.* Illus. by Nicholas Mordvinoff. New York: Harcourt Brace Jovanovich, Inc., 1953.

Little, Mary E. *1, 2, 3 for the Library.* Illus. by the author. New York: Atheneum Publishers, 1974.

Livermore, Elaine. *Find the Cat.* Illus. by the author. Boston: Houghton Mifflin Co., 1973.

Lobel, Arnold. *Frog and Toad Are Friends.* Illus. by the author. New York: Harper & Row Publishers, Inc., 1970.

———. *Giant John.* Illus. by the author. New York: Harper & Row Publishers, Inc., 1964.

———. *Prince Bertram the Bad.* Illus. by the author. New York: Harper & Row Publishers, Inc., 1963.

———. *A Zoo for Mr. Muster.* Illus. by the author. New York: Harper & Row Publishers, Inc., 1962.

Lund, Doris. *You Ought to See Herbert's House.* Illus. by Steven Kellogg. New York: Franklin Watts, Inc., 1973.

McCloskey, Robert. *Blueberries for Sal.* Illus. by the author. New York: Viking Press, Inc., 1948.

———. *Make Way for Ducklings.* Illus. by the author. New York: Viking Press, Inc., 1941.

McGovern, Ann. *Zoo, Where Are You?* Illus. by Ezra Jack Keats. New York: Harper & Row Publishers, Inc., 1964.

MacGregor, Ellen. *Theodore Turtle.* Illus. by Paul Galdone. New York: McGraw-Hill Book Co., 1955.

Mack, Stan. *10 Bears in My Bed.* Illus. by the author. New York: Pantheon Books, 1974.

McLeish, Kenneth. *Chicken Licken.* Illus. by Jutta Ash. Scarsdale, N.Y.: Bradbury Press, 1973.

Maestro, Giulio. *The Tortoise's Tug of War.* Illus. by the author. Scarsdale, N.Y.: Bradbury Press, 1971.

Mahy, Margaret. *A Lion in the Meadow.* Illus. by Jenny Williams. New York: Franklin Watts, Inc., 1969.

Marshall, James. *Yummers!* Illus. by the author. Boston: Houghton Mifflin Co., 1973.

Massie, Diane R. *Walter Was a Frog.* Illus. by the author. New York: Simon & Schuster, Inc., 1970.

Mayer, Mercer. *There's a Nightmare in My Closet.* Illus. by the author. New York: Dial Press, 1968.

Experiencing Literature

Miklowitz, Gloria. *The Zoo That Moved.* Illus. by Don Madden. Chicago: Follett Publishing Co., 1968.

Miller, Edna. *Mousekin's Golden House.* Illus. by the author. Englewood Cliffs, N.J.: Prentice-Hall, Inc., 1964.

Minarik, Else. *Little Bear.* Illus. by Maurice Sendak. New York: Harper & Row Publishers, Inc., 1957.

———. *The Little Giant Girl and the Elf Boy.* Illus. by Garth Williams. New York: Harper & Row Publishers, Inc., 1963.

Munari, Bruno. *Bruno Munari's Zoo.* Illus. by the author. New York: Collins-World Publishing Co., Inc., 1963.

Myers, Walter D. *The Dragon Takes a Wife.* Illus. by Ann Grifalconi. Indianapolis: Bobbs-Merrill Co., Inc., 1972.

Ness, Evaline. *Sam, Bangs, and Moonshine.* Illus. by the author. New York: Holt, Rinehart & Winston, Inc., 1972.

Nixon, Joan. *The Alligator under the Bed.* Illus. by Jan Hughes. New York: G. P. Putnam's Sons, 1974.

Nodset, Joan. *Who Took the Farmer's Hat?* Illus. by Fritz Siebel. Eau Claire, Wis.: E. M. Hale & Company, 1963.

Peppe, Rodney. *Circus Numbers.* Illus. by the author. New York: Delacorte Press, 1969.

Petersham, Maud. *The Box with Red Wheels.* Illus. by Maud and Miska Petersham. New York: Macmillan Publishing Co., Inc., 1949.

Piper, Watty. *The Little Engine That Could.* Illus. by the author. Eau Claire, Wis.: E. M. Hale & Company, 1954.

Pomerantz, Charlotte. *The Piggy in the Puddle.* Illus. by James Marshall. New York: Macmillan Publishing Co., Inc., 1974.

Potter, Beatrix. *The Tale of Peter Rabbit.* Illus. by the author. New York: Frederick Warne & Co., Inc., 1902.

Poulet, Virginia. *Blue Bug's Vegetable Garden.* Illus. by Donald Charles. Chicago: Children's Press, 1973.

Preston, Edna. *One Dark Night.* Illus. by Kurt Werth. New York: Viking Press, Inc., 1969.

Purdy, Susan. *If You Have a Yellow Lion.* Illus. by the author. Philadelphia: J. B. Lippincott Co., 1966.

Reiss, John J. *Colors.* Illus. by the author. Scarsdale, N.Y.: Bradbury Press, 1969.

———. *Numbers.* Illus. by the author. Scarsdale, N.Y.: Bradbury Press, 1971.

Rey, Hans A. *Curious George.* Illus. by the author. Boston: Houghton Mifflin Co., 1941.

Rey, Margaret. *Curious George Flies a Kite.* Illus. by Hans A. Rey. Boston: Houghton Mifflin Co., 1958.

Rice, Inez. *The March Wind.* Illus. by Vladimir Bobri. New York: Lothrop, Lee & Shepard Co., 1957.

Ross, Geraldine. *Scat, the Witch's Cat.* Illus. by Kurt Werth. New York: McGraw-Hill Book Co., 1958.

Sauer, Julia. *Mike's House.* Illus. by Don Freeman. New York: Viking Press, Inc., 1954.

Scheer, Julian. *Rain Makes Applesauce.* Illus. by Marvin Bileck. New York: Holiday House, Inc., 1964.

Seignobosc, Francoise. *Jeanne-Marie Counts Her Sheep.* Illus. by the author. New York: Charles Scribner's Sons, 1957.

Sendak, Maurice. *One Was Johnny.* Illus. by the author. New York: Harper & Row Publishers, Inc., 1962.

———. *Pierre.* Illus. by the author. New York: Harper & Row Publishers, Inc., 1962.

———. *Where the Wild Things Are.* Illus. by the author. New York: Harper & Row Publishers, Inc., 1963.

Seuss, Dr. *The 500 Hats of Bartholomew Cubbins.* Illus. by the author. Eau Claire, Wis.: E. M. Hale & Company, 1938.

———. *Horton Hatches the Egg.* Illus. by the author. New York: Random House, Inc., 1954.

———. *Yertle the Turtle, and Other Stories.* Illus. by the author. New York: Random House, Inc., 1958.

Shaw, Richard. *The Kitten in the Pumpkin Patch.* Illus. by Jacqueline Kahane. New York: Frederick Warne & Co., Inc., 1973.

Sheldon, Aure. *Fit for a King.* Illus. by Robert Sweetland. Minneapolis: Carolrhoda Books, Inc., 1974.

Silverstein, Shel. *The Giving Tree.* Illus. by the author. New York: Harper & Row Publishers, Inc., 1964.

Simon, Sidney. *Henry, the Uncatchable Mouse.* Illus. by Nola Langner. New York. W. W. Norton & Co., Inc., 1964.

Sivulich, Sandra. *I'm Going on a Bear Hunt.* Illus. by Glen Rounds. New York: E. P. Dutton & Co., Inc., 1973.

Skorpen, Liesel. *All the Lassies.* Illus. by Bruce M. Scott. New York: Dial Press, 1970.

Slobodkin, Louis. *Trick or Treat.* Illus. by the author. New York: Macmillan Publishing Co., Inc., 1967.

Slobodkina, Esphyr. *Caps for Sale.* Illus. by the author. Reading, Pa.: Addison-Wesley Publishing Co., Inc., 1947.

Spier, Peter. *The Fox Went Out on a Chilly Night.* New York: Doubleday & Co., Inc., 1961.

Steig, William. *Amos and Boris.* Illus. by the author. New York: Farrar, Straus & Giroux, Inc., 1971.

Experiencing Literature

Steiner, Charlotte. *My Slippers Are Red.* Illus. by the author. New York: Alfred A. Knopf, Inc., 1957.
Swift, Hildegarde. *The Little Red Lighthouse and the Great Gray Bridge.* Illus. by Lynd Ward. New York: Harcourt Brace Jovanovich, Inc., 1942.
Thayer, Jane. *Gus Was a Friendly Ghost.* Illus. by Seymour Fleishman. New York: William Morrow & Co., Inc., 1962.
Titus, Eve. *Anatole.* Illus. by Paul Galdone. New York: McGraw-Hill Book Co., 1956.
Tolstoy, Alexei. *The Great Big Enormous Turnip.* Illus. by Helen Oxenbury. New York: Franklin Watts, Inc., 1969.
Tresselt, Alvin. *White Snow, Bright Snow.* Illus. by Roger Duvoisin. New York: Lothrop, Lee & Shepard, Inc., 1947.
Tudor, Tasha. *Skiddycock Pond.* Illus. by the author. New York: J. B. Lippincott Co., 1965.
Udry, Janice. *The Moon Jumpers.* Illus. by Maurice Sendak. New York: Harper & Row Publishers, Inc., 1959.
———. *A Tree Is Nice.* Illus. by Marc Simont. New York: Harper & Row Publishers, Inc., 1956.
Ungerer, Tomi. *Crictor.* Illus. by the author. New York: Harper & Row Publishers, Inc., 1958.
Varga, Judy. *The Dragon Who Liked to Spit Fire.* Illus. by the author. New York: William Morrow & Co., Inc., 1961.
Viorst, Judith. *Alexander and the Terrible, Horrible, No Good, Very Bad Day.* Illus. by Ray Cruz. New York: Atheneum Publishers, 1972.
———. *My Mama Says There Aren't Any Zombies, Ghosts, Vampires, Creatures, Demons, Monsters, Fiends, Goblins or Things.* Illus. by Kay Chorao. New York: Atheneum Publishers, 1973.
Vipont, Elfrida. *The Elephant and the Baby.* Illus. by Raymond Briggs. New York: Coward, McCann & Geoghegan, Inc., 1970.
Waber, Bernard. *The House on East 88th Street.* Illus. by the author. Boston: Houghton Mifflin Co., 1962.
———. *Lovable Lyle.* Illus. by the author. Boston: Houghton Mifflin Co., 1969.
———. *Lyle and the Happy Birthday Party.* Illus. by the author. Boston: Houghton Mifflin Co., 1966.
———. *Lyle, Lyle Crocodile.* Illus. by the author. Boston: Houghton Mifflin Co., 1965.
———. *Rich Cat, Poor Cat.* Illus. by the author. Boston: Houghton Mifflin Co., 1963.
Wahl, Jan. *Margaret's Birthday.* Illus. by Mercer Mayer. New York: Four Winds Press, 1971.

Withers, Carl. *The Tale of a Black Cat.* Illus. by Alan Cober. New York: Holt, Rinehart & Winston, Inc., 1966.

Wolkstein, Diane. *Cool Ride in the Sky.* Illus. by Paul Galdone. New York: Random House, Inc., 1973.

Yashima, Taro. *Umbrella.* Illus. by the author. New York: Viking Press, Inc., 1958.

Zemach, Harve. *The Judge.* Illus. by Margot Zemach. New York: Farrar, Straus & Giroux, Inc., 1969.

Zimnik, Reiner. *The Bear on the Motorcycle.* Illus. by the author. New York: Atheneum Publishers, 1963.

Zion, Gene. *Harry, the Dirty Dog.* Illus. by Margaret B. Graham. New York: Harper & Row Publishers, Inc., 1956.

Zolotow, Charlotte. *The Bunny Who Found Easter.* Illus. by Betty F. Peterson. Berkeley, Calif.: Parnassus Press, 1959.

———. *Mr. Rabbit and the Lovely Present.* Illus. by Maurice Sendak. New York: Harper & Row Publishers, Inc., 1962.

———. *My Friend John.* Illus. by Ben Shecter. New York: Harper & Row Publishers, Inc., 1968.

———. *The Summer Night.* Illus. by Ben Shecter. New York: Harper & Row Publishers, Inc., 1974.

———. *A Tiger Called Thomas.* Illus. by Kurt Werth. New York: Lothrop, Lee & Shepard Co., 1963.

Poetry Books Cited

Aldis, Florence. *Highdays and Holidays.* Illus. by Emma L. Brock. New York: E. P. Dutton & Co., 1927.

———. *All Together.* Illus. by Helen D. Jameson. New York: G. P. Putnam's Sons, 1952.

———, *Everything and Anything.* Illus. by Helen D. Jameson. New York: Minton, Balch & Co., 1927.

———. *Here, There, and Everywhere.* Illus. by Marjorie Flack. New York: Minton, Balch & Co., 1928.

Arbuthnot, May Hill. *Time for Poetry.* Illus. by Arthur Paul. Chicago: Scott, Foresman & Co., 1952.

Association for Childhood Education International. *Sung under the Silver Umbrella.* Illus. by Dorothy Lathrop. New York: Macmillan Publishing Co., Inc., 1935.

Brewton, John Edmund. *Under the Tent of the Sky.* Illus. by Robert Lawson. New York: Macmillan Publishing Co., Inc., 1937.

Brewton, Sara. *Birthday Candles Burning Bright.* Illus. by Vera Brock. New York: Macmillan Publishing Co., Inc., 1960.

Experiencing Literature

———. *Bridled with Rainbows.* Illus. by Vera Brock. New York: Macmillan Publishing Co., Inc., 1949.

Burroughs, Margaret Taylor. *Did You Feed My Cow?* Illus. by Joe E. De Velasco. Chicago: Follett Publishing Co., 1969.

Carlson, Bernice Wells. *Listen! And Help Tell the Story.* Illus. by Burmah Burris. Nashville: Abingdon Press, 1965.

Chute, Marchette. *Rhymes about Us.* Illus. by the author. New York: E. P. Dutton & Co., 1974.

Cole, William. *Beastly Boys and Ghastly Girls.* Illus. by Tomi Ungerer. New York: Collins-World Publishing Co., 1964.

———. *Oh, That's Ridiculous!* Illus. by Tomi Ungerer. New York: Viking Press, Inc., 1972.

Fisher, Aileen. *Cricket in a Thicket.* Illus. by Feodor Rojankovsky. New York: Charles Scribner's Sons, 1963.

———. *In One Door and out the Other.* Illus. by Lillian Hoban. New York: Thomas Y. Crowell Company, Inc., 1969.

Harrington, Mildred P. *Ring-a-Round.* Illus. by Corydon Bell. New York: Macmillan Publishing Co., Inc., 1930.

Hubbell, Patricia. *Catch Me a Wind.* Illus. by Susan Trommler. New York: Atheneum Publishers, 1968.

Huffard, Grace Thompson. *My Poetry Book.* Illus. by Willy Pogany. New York: Holt, Rinehart & Winston, Inc., 1956.

Hughes, Langston. *Don't You Turn Back.* Illus. by Ann Grifalconi. New York: Alfred A. Knopf, Inc., 1969.

Ireson, Barbara. *The Barnes Book of Nursery Verse.* Illus. by George Adamson. New York: Barnes & Noble, Inc., 1960.

Jacobs, Leland. *Is Somewhere Always Far Away?* Illus. by John E. Johnson. New York: Holt, Rinehart & Winston, Inc., 1967.

Larrick, Nancy. *Poetry for Holidays.* Illus. by Kelly Oechsli. Champaign, Ill.: Garrard Publishing Co., 1966.

McCord, David. *Away and Ago.* Illus. by Leslie Morrill. Boston: Little, Brown & Co., 1974.

McEwen, Catherine Schaefer. *Away We Go!* Illus. by Barbara Cooney. New York: Thomas Y. Crowell Company, Inc., 1956.

Mannheim, Grete. *Feather or Fur.* Photographs by the author. New York: Alfred A. Knopf, Inc., 1967.

Merriam, Eve. *Catch a Little Rhyme.* Illus. by Imero Gobbato. New York: Atheneum Publishers, 1966.

———. *There Is No Rhyme for Silver.* Illus. by Joseph Schindelman. New York: Atheneum Publishers, 1962.

Milne, A. A. *Now We Are Six.* Illus. by Ernest Shepard. New York: E. P. Dutton & Co., 1927.

Nash, Ogden. *The Moon Is Shining Bright as Day.* Illus. by Rose Shirvanian. Philadelphia: J. B. Lippincott Co., 1953.

Neville, Mary. *Woody and Me.* Illus. by Ronni Solert. New York: Pantheon Books, 1966.

One, Two, Buckle My Shoe; a Book of Counting Rhymes. Illus. by Gail Haley. New York: Doubleday & Co., Inc., 1964.

O'Neill, Mary. *Hailstones and Halibut Bones.* Illus. by Leonard Weisgard. New York: Doubleday & Co., Inc., 1961.

Peterson, Isabel J. *The First Book of Poetry.* Illus. by Kathleen Elgin. New York: Franklin Watts, Inc., 1954.

Prelutsky, Jack. *The Pack Rat's Day.* Illus. by Margaret Bloy Graham. New York: Macmillan Publishing Co., Inc., 1974.

Rawlins, Margaret G. *Round about Six.* Illus. by Denis Wrigley. New York: Frederick Warne, Inc., 1973.

Richards, Laura. *Tirra Lirra.* Illus. by Marguerite Davis. Boston: Little, Brown & Co., 1955.

Rojankovsky, Feodor. *Tall Book of Mother Goose.* New York: Harper & Row Publishers, Inc., 1942.

Rossetti, Christina. *Sing-Song.* Illus. by Marguerite Davis. New York: Macmillan Publishing Co., Inc., 1924.

Shaw, Richard, comp. *The Fox Book.* Illus. by various artists. New York: Frederick Warne, Inc., 1971.

———. *The Frog Book.* Illus. by various artists. New York: Frederick Warne, Inc., 1972.

Silverstein, Shel. *Where the Sidewalk Ends.* Illus. by the author. New York: Harper & Row Publishers, Inc., 1974.

Stevenson, Robert Louis. *A Child's Garden of Verses.* Illus. by Alexander Dobkin. New York: Collins-World Publishing Co., Inc., 1946.

Tippett, James S. *Crickety-Cricket!* Illus. by Mary Chalmers. New York: Harper & Row Publishers, Inc., 1973.

Untermeyer, Louis, sel. *The Golden Treasury of Poetry.* Illus. by Joan Walsh Anglund. Racine, Wis.: Golden Press, 1959.

Vance, Eleanor Graham. *From Little to Big.* Illus. by June Goldsborough. Chicago: Follett Publishing Co., 1972.

Werner, Jane. *The Golden Book of Poetry.* Illus. by Gertrude Elliott. Racine, Wis.: Golden Press, 1949.

Sharing Literature with Children

by Carol Sue Peterson

Sharing Literature with Children," a program conducted by the Children's Department of the Orlando (Florida) Public Library, emphasizes community involvement in providing children with positive literature experiences. Established in 1971, the program was an outgrowth of a study to determine how the public library could provide meaningful literature experiences for all the children in the library district. Basically, it operates on the premise that since library staff members cannot reach each child individually, they should concentrate on teaching adults and teen-agers who work with children the importance of sharing literature with them.

After four years of top priority status in the Children's Department, "Sharing Literature with Children" has made a noticeable impression upon the community. Nearly 12,000 adults and teen-agers have participated in the program, and many of these persons are using their skills with children on a regular basis.

In order to teach the adults in the community how to share literature with children, the library staff prepared a workshop to be held for existing agencies, institutions, and organizations in their own meeting places. The workshop, flexible in length, can be expanded into an all-day program or condensed into a 20-minute presentation. In the workshop, the staff demonstrates storytelling techniques, puppetry, use of the flannel board, finger plays, and audiovisual literature productions. Kits of resource materials have been put together, including samples of picture books, simple puppets, characters for the flannel board, and audio-visual materials and equipment.

Featured in the workshop are books, other media and equipment that can

Carol Sue Peterson is Head of the Children's Department, Orlando Public Library, Orlando, Florida.

be checked out at the library, and simple, inexpensive items that can be prepared from household odds and ends. Some of the items featured include puppets made from wire coat hangers, styrofoam balls, and other materials; flannel boards made from cardboard boxes and cheap outing flannel; and flannel board characters from magazines, discarded books, coloring books, and so on.

To provide reinforcement for workshop participants, the staff compiled a sixty-four-page manual consisting of instructions for making puppets and other story materials; lists of books, films, filmstrips, records, and posters dealing with children's literature; and a collection of finger plays. This book is distributed free of charge to any person attending a "Sharing Literature with Children" workshop.

The most efficient method of reaching adults who work with children is to work through organized agencies and institutions within the community. So it was necessary to identify such groups and establish some lines of communication. Lists were compiled of churches, scout leaders, day care centers, service organizations, parent groups, public and private schools, volunteer groups, and so forth. Brochures announcing the "Sharing Literature with Children" workshops were mailed to representatives of the various agencies. Later, staff members called or visited these groups to explain further the sharing-literature concept.

Slowly, community groups have volunteered to participate in the program. Each time a workshop is scheduled for a group, a team of two librarians transports the kits of materials and equipment out to the group. Since many of the participants are not regular library users, the staff must concentrate on the quality of the initial meeting, for the success of the program depends greatly on the early establishment of a comfortable rapport. Because the attendees range from semi-literate parents to professional educators, the method of presentation must be custom tailored for each group. Research on the group prior to the presentation determines the length of the workshop as well as the depth and the content.

In the past four years the library has conducted about 600 workshops attended by nearly 12,000 adults and teen-agers. Since workshops average one hour in length, it is quite safe to assume that the 600 hours spent in workshops has affected a vast number of children whose lives might otherwise never be touched by the library. In fact, some specific situations have been dramatic success stories. For example, two years ago the staff visited a day care center licensed to house 300 children. Nowhere in sight were books, toys, or materials of any kind. All that could be seen were tots milling around, mostly with thumbs in their mouths. According to a counselor, the local guidance clinic had been unable to get successful I.Q. scores on these children because they simply could not verbalize. The library team spent an hour talking to the aides about the importance of sharing stories with the children and left

325 paperback picture books with them for an indefinite period of time. Nine months later the director of the center called the library asking for help in teaching the aides some in-depth skills in storytelling and related arts. Recently when staff members visited the center unannounced, the aides were in the middle of what they considered a routine story hour complete with a puppet show. The nursery teachers bring the children to visit the public library several times a year; these youngsters excitedly look at books and listen to stories— but more important, they *talk* about the books and stories.

Even school faculties often need to be encouraged to share more literature with children. While most teachers know how to tell stories, many just do not include storytelling as a regular activity. After a 30-minute workshop, one school developed an exciting program almost immediately. Sixth-grade language arts classes began telling stories to kindergarten and first-grade classes. These sixth graders also wrote plays, made puppets, and performed puppet shows for the little ones. In this way, the older children were given the opportunity to develop both written and oral language skills and the younger ones were further exposed to stories.

In another instance, a women's service organization participated in a workshop, and afterwards arranged to present puppet shows to the general public and to Head Start groups in the nearest branch library during alternate weeks. As a result the children in that community have been exposed to literature sharing with a regularity that the small branch staff or the main library Children's Department simply could not provide.

In still another successful case, a workshop was held for a group of high school students enrolled in a day care aide training program. Approximately a month after the workshop the entire class came to the library to reexamine the sample puppets and to request help in constructing their own puppets. The students then wrote puppet shows based on favorite stories and presented them to the children in a day care center. This particular center had already participated in a workshop and had implemented its own program with puppets, flannel board stories, books, and audio-visual materials checked out from the library.

And so it goes. Example after example could be listed and described but basically the same pattern emerges. It is particularly significant that in the disadvantaged areas, it is usually the library staff who makes the first move by initiating the workshop program and by taking it out of the building directly to the persons involved. It is up to the library staff to establish a warm rapport and to emphasize that they are working with the participants for the common good of all children. After this initial contact and perhaps one or two follow-up contacts, probably in the form of story hours or puppet shows for the children, participants usually begin to take advantage of the total resources of the library.

Sharing Literature with Children

The concept of conducting storytelling workshops is not new for public libraries. The unique feature of the Orlando Public Library program is its relative priority among all the services in the Children's Department, for the program ranks even above direct service to children. Since an hour spent working with ten adults will ultimately provide more children with regular literature experiences than an hour spent telling stories to ten children, the workshop program takes precedence. Predictably, as the "Sharing Literature with Children" program has grown and flourished, demands for direct services in the main and branch libraries have increased.

The program, besides providing a valuable community service, has proved to be an excellent public relations medium. During the four years since its inception, over 350 different agencies have participated in workshops. The public library is now a familiar place to members of these groups. Television, radio, and newspaper media have been generous in advertising "Sharing Literature with Children," thus bringing the library to the attention of an even wider range of citizens.

To help explain the importance of community involvement in sharing literature with children, the Orlando Public Library has produced for distribution the following audio-visual materials:

"Sharing Literature with Children" multimedia kit containing a sound filmstrip, SLWC manual, and a packet of tips for setting up a similar program. Distributed by the Orlando Public Library, 10 N. Rosalind, Orlando, Florida 32801 .....$24.95

"Sharing Literature with Children" 16mm color sound film describing the SLWC program, including tips for setting up a similar one. Running time: 16 minutes. Produced by Cypress Films, Carmel, California. Distributed by Orlando Public Library, 10 N. Rosalind, Orlando, Florida 32801 .. $195.00

Funding

Local funding	January 1971 to July 1975	$113,534.00
LSCA program grant	July 1971 to July 1972	29,460.00
LSCA program grant	July 1972 to July 1973	18,581.00
Florida State Library program grant	July 1973 to July 1974	35,000.00
LSCA program grant	July 1974 to July 1975	12,000.00

A large portion of the first Library Services and Construction Act (LSCA) grant provided salaries for an additional two full-time and one part-time positions which, subsequently, were incorporated into the local budget. Funds were also used to purchase filmstrip projectors, cassette players, 8mm sound cartridge projectors, and appropriate audio-visual literature presentations to be checked out by workshop participants. A portion of the funds purchased paperback picture books that were distributed on long-term loan to day care centers and Head Start centers. The manuals, given free to each workshop participant, were reproduced with LSCA funds. The F75 grant was used to purchase collections of audio-visual equipment and materials to be placed in branch libraries for easy access by persons in the community.

From a monetary standpoint, an important feature of "Sharing Literature with Children" is that the program is completely flexible. It can be developed on a very limited scale or a very large one. As many or as few staff members and as much or as little equipment and materials can be used as a library wishes to commit to the program. The size of the library and the extent of its commitment to the project are the determining factors.

Dial-a-Story

by Linda J. Geistlinger

Would you like to reach every child in your community with stories from your library? Consider the telephone!

Dial-a-Story, a program that gives preschool children a special listening experience, was planned as an impact item to draw attention to the Early Childhood Project of the San Francisco Public Library. Designed to meet a community need for information about young children and early childhood materials, the Early Childhood Project provides a multimedia collection about and for use with preschoolers. As a component of the project, Dial-a-Story is

As the goal of the San Francisco Public Library Early Childhood Project, which she designed, Effie Lee Morris envisioned providing adults with information about the preschool child and the resources available for use with this age group. A reference collection to support adults in parenting and specialized staff were selected to help implement this project in Children's Services—service to the preschool child and to the adult involved in his care.

Beginning in 1972, Miss Morris and her staff have worked on a city-wide level with individuals and with city agencies and groups. The staff provides in service training and support for children's librarians. One staff member conducts on-site programs for the residents of three housing projects whose populations are Chinese, black and Spanish-speaking. A growing community-information referral file has proved a much needed and appreciated resource.

Two features of the Early Childhood Project are described in this publication: "Parenting Collection" by Grace Ruth, and "Dial-a-Story" by Linda Geistlinger. The parent reference collection in the Early Childhood Project room proved to be so useful to both the general public and the children's librarians that similar collections were selected for the Main Children's Room and the library branches. Dial-a-Story was a segment of the program planned as an impact item to draw attention to the project. It has been widely and successfully copied.—*Editor.*

Linda J. Geistlinger is Children's Specialist, Early Education Project, San Francisco Public Library.

Experiencing Literature

a totally aural complement to the important experience of sharing literature with young children.

Dial-a-Story is a program of 3-minute recordings of stories, poems, and songs selected for children ages two through five years. Two telephone lines are in operation twenty-four hours every day, both carrying the same story. The recordings are changed at the beginning of each week. Children dial 626-6516. If the line is busy, the call is automatically switched over to 626-6517. Only the 626-6516 number is publicized.

Publicity

Bookmarks, which invite children to "Dial-a-Story," were designed and printed in English, Spanish, and Chinese. Text: "If you are 2, 3, 4, or 5 you can hear stories and poems. Dial 626-6516. Dial-a-Story." In addition, the Chinese and Spanish texts inform children that the stories are told in English. The bookmarks were widely distributed through the Main Children's Room, the Bookmobile, all branch library Children's Rooms, and to preschool agencies and city-wide agencies working with preschoolers, as well as to newspapers, radio, and TV stations.

Mechanics

Two Bell System 100A Automatic Answering Systems are being used. Each system consists of a telephone and a box about $9'' \times 9'' \times 18''$ in size, which are easily stored on shelves in the Early Childhood Project office. Each machine contains a three-minute tape. Stories are recorded by speaking directly into the telephone receiver. When a new recording is made, the previous one is erased from the tape. With two machines, the story must be recorded on each machine separately. The tape stops automatically at the end of three minutes so that the phone line will not be tied up by one child. Several other types of recording systems are available, some that use cassette tapes. Depending upon the type of equipment chosen, costs will vary. In San Francisco, the current monthly service charge for each line is approximately $25, in addition to the initial installation costs. Check with your local telephone company representative if a similar program is being considered.

In over two years of operation, there have been few problems with the Dial-a-Story equipment, even though it has been in almost constant use daily. Cleaning, repair, or replacement of the recording device is occasionally necessary. There has been no reported problem of lines being overloaded or jammed due to Dial-a-Story, as has been the case elsewhere in the country, although a telephone company representative had assured us this would happen.

Selection of Materials

Prepared and recorded by the project librarians, material is selected that can be read in approximately 2 minutes, 45 seconds, or can be adapted to that time span without making great changes in the language and story line of the original. The text must stand on its own, not relying on any accompanying illustrations to tell the story. Much of the material selected is in the public domain, such as folktales and nursery rhymes. The recording usually ends with a suggestion of something the listener can do that relates to the story.

Persons interested in beginning a similar program have asked if the telephone recording of stories has had a negative effect on attendance at the library's preschool story hour. The experience has been that children who are ardent fans of Dial-a-Story regularly attend preschool story hour and other programs in their own libraries. Often at the end of a recording the listener is encouraged to come to the library with family and friends. Some parents and children come asking specifically for titles being used on Dial-a-Story because they like to read the story before or after they hear it on the telephone. One children's librarian reported that the regular members of her preschool story hour group did not always remember their home telephone numbers, but each of them knew the Dial-a-Story number! For children who may not be able to come to the library for story hour, Dial-a-Story provides one way for them to enjoy good stories.

The great number of unanswered calls (approximately 10,000 busy signals were counted by the telephone company within a one-week period) shows the tremendous popularity of Dial-a-Story in the San Francisco area. A frequent comment is, "The line is always busy," indicating that more than two lines are desirable, if the budget allows.

Continuing evaluative response to Dial-a-Story by children and adults is very positive. Here are a few comments received during one period of evaluation:

"We love it as a family! The children love it and like to do it with friends who are visiting."

"My son (4 years) likes the idea of a story over the phone, and most of them he knows, so it does hold his interest."

"She (6 years) usually calls several times a week, usually enjoys the stories. Pleased when she finds the book in the library later."

"Excellent project—hope it will be continued. My children enjoy Dial-a-Story as much for the opportunity of using the telephone with some independence, as they enjoy the stories themselves."

And this comment seems to sum it all up (translated from Spanish):

"First of all, please excuse my writing in Spanish. My English is very poor. Having picked up your flyer giving your number 626-6516, I

began calling regularly so that my children could participate in your good program; such a wonderful gift to San Francisco children. I have two at home. They and I listen to your stories in English, myself in order to help me learn the language. Having started to work at a clothing factory about a month and a half ago, I spread the word among my Latino-American co-workers, and now many of them call your number and listen to your program....
P.S. I have been in San Francisco only two months."

Since its beginning in February 1973, Dial-a-Story has been a highly successful program, much appreciated and enjoyed by thousands of preschoolers, older children, and many adults who also Dial-a-Story.

Emergency!

by Jane Granstrom

A state of emergency exists in any library when the children's librarian calls in sick on the morning of a picture book story hour. Such a situation creates a real dilemma for any library administrator committed to consistent programming for preschoolers but lacking an assistant in the children's room, volunteers, or ready access to a film collection. Nor is the sick call the only kind of programming emergency that can occur. There are film programs that go awry as the audience looks on—and waits. There are the suddenly announced or unexpected field trips from local nursery schools and day care centers. And there are the last-minute needs and desperate requests for help that issue from individuals or community groups who work with preschoolers.

In response to just such emergencies, the children's department of the Thomas Crane Public Library in Quincy, Massachusetts, developed a program resource collection. The collection is for use within the library system (which includes seven branch libraries), and outside the library by students and teachers in early childhood education, by nursery schools and day care centers, and by other community agencies and adults working with children.

The resource materials available in the collection include commercially prepared program kits, felt board stories, non-commercial materials designed by the staff, filmstrips, recordings, pictures, and books about program techniques and activities. The recordings include sound effects, singing games, and RCA's eight Dance-a-Story storybook/cassette combinations. The bulk of the filmstrip collection is taken directly from picture books. The felt board stories are adapted from picture book stories that have been popular with pre-

Jane Granstrom is Supervisor of Children's Services, Thomas Crane Public Library, Quincy, Massachusetts.

school audiences. The collection of pictures includes Brian Wildsmith teaching cards, Mother Goose picture sets, and a set of tell-and-draw stories. *Kaleidoscope: Programs for Children* are commercially prepared program kits that include a detailed program guide, materials for use in the program, a bibliography of materials related to the program theme, descriptions of related activities, and suggestions for preschool programs. The programs are lively and invite the active participation of the children.

The special feature of the program resource collection, however, is the preschool emergency kits. Because the picture book story hours for preschoolers were consistently well attended and promoted a consistently high rate of book borrowing, it seemed essential to hold these programs without fail. Also, most community groups or individuals that turned to Quincy's public library for help in preparing activities were dealing with preschoolers. These package programs are ready for use at a moment's notice; therefore, the kits are particularly useful in situations when time and limited experience are determining factors.

The initial seven preschool emergency kits were painstakingly developed. First, staff members selected subjects that had broad appeal, that were conducive to a variety of activities, and about which a number of recommended picture books had been written. One of the first subjects selected was animals, and because of the great number of good picture books available and the high interest in the topic, it was divided into two programs, "Animal Parade" and "Birds." Since Quincy is a seacoast city with twenty-seven miles of waterfront, "At the Beach" seemed to be a program topic that capitalized on local interest. Many of the youngsters attending picture book hours come with a little friend, and as the series of story hours progresses new friendships are formed. The kit, "Friends," reflects friendship as a real concern of childhood. "Ghosts and Goblins" speaks for itself, offering the thrill of a scare tempered by the security of a friendly group! Neither "Ghosts and Goblins" nor "Snowy Days" needs to be strictly seasonal, although both are topics with special appeal at holiday time. "What's Cooking?" is the most ambitious of the emergency kits and one of the most enjoyable. Young children seem to relish participating in a traditionally "adult" activity, creating a "mess" with cooking utensils and ingredients, and eating the results of their handiwork.

Once the topics were selected, lists of picture books were drawn up for each topic. Criteria for final selection included: (1) availability in paperback, (2) contribution of the titles to the progression of the program, and (3) ease of familiarization with previously unfamiliar titles. Final selection provided a minimum of four paperback picture books for each topic.

Using the books as the foundation for the emergency kit, a half dozen activities were developed around the central theme. Each activity was outlined fully. Any activity calling for special materials was carefully considered before inclusion. Cost factors, availability of materials, and the potential for reuse had to be weighed. Then the kits were ready for testing. Some were used during the regular picture book hour schedule. Some were used with visiting day care and nursery school groups. Some were used in part, and some completely. All were used more than once, under different circumstances, and by different people; with each use there were adjustments and refinements.

In addition to the program outline in each kit packet, the text and directions for finger plays, games, songs, and poems are supplied. As a precaution, only photocopies of text and directions are supplied with the kits. The original copies of outlines, finger plays, games, and so forth are kept in a program resource file for replacement purposes. The program outline for each subject notes the sources from which activities come, and when a source is used repeatedly a copy is placed in the program resource book collection. For instance, Grayson's *Let's Do Fingerplays* (Robert B. Luce) has been a source of activities used not only in the emergency kits but also in other program efforts, so there is a copy in the circulating collection of the children's department and one in the program resource collection.

The program "Snowy Days" suggests cutting out snowflakes as a craft activity. The emergency kit supplies the instructions and squares of paper for the activity. Each time that kit is returned to the resource collection, the supply of squares must be replenished. In selecting activities such as this one, two factors were kept in mind. The first was that any materials required by the activity could be supplied in the kit, as the paper squares are, or could be easily obtained (most agencies working with children have small scissors on hand). The second factor was that the activities could be done at home with materials on hand. It seemed essential that the experiences offered by these programs extend themselves beyond the immediate circumstances in which they were presented.

The program "Animal Parade" includes a Dance-a-Story cassette entitled "Noah's Ark." The Dance-a-Story recordings invite pantomime, creative rhythm, and beginning dance techniques. In this particular program the Dance-a-Story gives children a chance to pretend to be the various animals they have been hearing about during the program. This activity requires a cassette player. We have found that most groups have their own equipment, preferring to allocate funds for the initial expense and then borrow from the library materials to use with the equipment. The resource collection does have its own cassette players and filmstrip projectors which are cord (not battery) operated. Both are loaned only within the library system. Cassettes rather than recordings were chosen; the staff hoped for greater durability and was sure of greater portability. As in the case of filmstrips, cassettes must always be checked upon return to be sure they have been rewound properly.

Program running time is a minimum of thirty minutes. Each program out-

Experiencing Literature

line refers to additional materials in the program resource collection that can be used in that program. "Ghosts and Goblins" suggests using the filmstrip *Georgie*. "What's Cooking?" suggests either the filmstrip *Stone Soup* or a felt board story based upon *Stone Soup*. Since the additional materials suggested in the program outlines circulate independently, they are not always available. Another vital feature of the program outline is the list of picture books related to the subject. The materials in the kit cannot be circulated to members of the audience. Yet at the library, it is this very circulation that we're trying to encourage. Therefore, each kit has a list of titles in the book collection that can be displayed or mentioned briefly—books that can be borrowed.

Because this project was experimental in concept, processing has been kept simple. Usage and needs may require a more sophisticated system. With the exception of the hardcover books that are processed by the catalog department, there is no cataloging of materials in the program resource collection. A book card is typed for each filmstrip, emergency kit, or recording and includes this information: a heading in red capitals—PROGRAM RESOURCE COLLEC.; the title of the article, such as *Preschool Emergency Kit: Animal Parade;* and the kind of material, such as filmstrip with booklet or felt board story. Each emergency kit lists the number of paperbacks, printed sheets, and any other materials, for example: 5 paperbacks, 3 printed sheets, 1 storybook/cassette.

The hardcover books in the program resource collection have entries in both the adult and the juvenile card catalogs. Other materials in the collection have unofficial entries in the juvenile card catalog only. These entries are typed on green cards that contrast with all other cards in the catalog. All entries are preceded by a card which states *Program Resource Collection,* where the material is stored, and the seven-day circulation period. The entries themselves are listings of available titles under the type of material. For instance, sixty titles are listed under filmstrips, seven titles are listed under preschool emergency kits.

The project is so new that there have been no complications resulting from lost or discarded materials. All materials are labeled PRC and stamped with the library name. The preschool emergency kits circulate in plastic bags as do the filmstrips, cassettes, and *Kaleidoscope* programs. The pictures and felt board stories circulate in large clasp envelopes.

The most significant cost factor in preparing the preschool emergency kits was staff time. The single most expensive item in any kit is the Dance-a-Story cassette. The paperbacks cost from under one dollar to under two dollars. Considering the potential use of these kits and the minimal processing involved, cost per kit is reasonable. Any additional materials, such as paperbacks, that become available will be added to the kits to give them greater breadth and flexibility.

Staff members are encouraged to fill out program reports, much like lesson plans, on their own story hours. After review and use by several staff members, these program plans become part of the resource collection. Some of these plans will be adapted for use as preschool emergency kit outlines.

Word-of-mouth is often the most effective form of library publicity, and this has been the case in promoting the use of the program resource collection. A descriptive brochure was prepared and mailed to community agencies working with children. The brochure, to be revised annually, is also given to anyone who borrows material from the collection.

These programs can act as a form of in-service training. Most of the program techniques used are basic to story hours for preschoolers and can be adapted to diverse subjects or themes. Not only are new staff members or story-hour substitutes given some very concrete guidelines for programming at this level, but they are enabled and encouraged to develop their own style and repertoires. Similarly, non-librarians involved in programming for young children can reap as many benefits as they have resources.

Obviously, the compilation of each kit represents several hours' work. But having the kits available means that a well-developed program is ready for use at very short notice and can be handled successfully by someone unfamiliar with programming. It means that a library is truly a resource within the community for the many groups and individuals who fall under the umbrella of outreach efforts. It means that one kind of library service, programming, is not subject to last-minute cancellations or dependent on the skills of one individual. In Quincy it means that we are closer to the ideal of "something for everybody."

Sample Preschool Emergency Kit:
Ghosts and Goblins

Chant: "The Dark House" from *Juba This and Juba That*, page 11—text supplied with kit. The leader will probably be asked to repeat this chant; we suggest the adult do it once or twice before having the children join in.

Storytelling: *A Woggle of Witches*—book supplied with kit. Take time to show the illustrations to your audience; they are particularly effective.

Game: "Pass the Witch's Broom"—broom supplied with kit. (The directions for making this broom are in *Let's Be Early Settlers with Daniel Boone*.) The broom is passed from hand to hand as long as there is music or the sound of your voice (you could read one of the stories, read a poem, etc.). When the sound stops whoever is holding the broom is a "witch."

Storytelling: *One Dark Night*—book supplied with kit. Read slowly, show pictures thoroughly.

Make-a-Witch: felt board activity—small felt board and felt pieces supplied with kit. Various features like noses, mouths, hair, eyes are placed on the felt board in various combinations to make different witches' faces. First demonstrate the activity imaginatively (you could give the witch a name, say where she's from and what she does). Then open the activity to the children, allowing them to take turns making a witch by combining features. Again, don't overextend the activity—it can be resumed informally after the program.

Picture book talk: *Georgie's Halloween, Magic People, Trick or Treat*—books supplied with kit. The pictures will aid you in describing the action of the story. Say just enough to whet interest.

If available, the following materials from the Program Resource Collection could be used in addition to or as substitutes for above activities: filmstrip *Georgie;* felt board story *The Humbug Witch.*

If possible, display books listed in the "Ghosts and Goblins" bibliography.

Examples from the Picture Book Collection for "Ghosts and Goblins"

Adams, Adrienne. *A Woggle of Witches.* New York: Charles Scribner's Sons, 1971.

Babbitt, Natalie. *The Something.* New York: Farrar, Straus & Giroux, Inc., 1970.

Balian, Lorna. *The Humbug Witch.* Nashville: Abingdon Press, 1965.

Benchley, Nathaniel. *A Ghost Named Fred.* New York: Harper & Row Publishers, Inc., 1968.

Bright, Robert. *Georgie* (several titles). New York: Doubleday & Co.

Calhoun, Mary. *The Witch of Hissing Hill.* New York: William Morrow & Co., 1964.

Carroll, Ruth. *The Witch Kitten.* New York: Henry Z. Walck, 1973.

Coombs, Patricia. *Dorrie* (several titles). New York: Lothrop, Lee & Shepard Co.

Devlin, Wende. *Old Black Witch.* New York: Parents' Magazine Press, 1966.

Embry, Margaret. *The Blue-Nosed Witch.* New York: Holiday House, Inc., 1956.

Freeman, Don. *Tilly Witch.* New York: Viking Press, 1969.

Glovach, Linda. *Little Witch* (several titles). Englewood Cliffs, N.J.: Prentice-Hall.

Hoff, Syd. *Mrs. Switch.* New York: G. P. Putnam's Sons, 1966.

Hurd, Edith. *The So-So Cat.* New York: Harper & Row Publishers, Inc., 1965.

Kettlekamp, Larry. *Spooky Magic.* New York: William Morrow & Co., 1955.

McGovern, Ann. *Squeals and Squiggles and Ghostly Giggles.* New York: Four Winds Press, 1973.

Preston, Edna. *One Dark Night.* New York: Viking Press, 1969.

Raskin, Ellen. *Ghost in a Four-Room Apartment.* New York: Atheneum Publishers, 1969.
Serraillier, Ian. *Suppose You Met a Witch.* Boston: Little, Brown & Co., 1973.
Tudor, Tasha. *Pumpkin Moonshine.* New York: Henry Z. Walck, 1938.
Unwin, Nora. *Two Too Many.* New York: David McKay, 1962.
Viorst, Judith. *My Mama Says There Aren't Any Zombies, Ghosts, Vampires, Creatures, Demons, Monsters, Fiends, Goblins, or Things.* New York: Atheneum Publishers, 1973.
Wyler, Rose. *Spooky Tricks.* New York: Harper & Row Publishers, Inc., 1968.
Zolotow, Charlotte. *A Tiger Called Thomas.* New York: Lothrop, Lee & Shepard Co., 1963.

Suppliers

Brian Wildsmith Teaching Cards: Franklin Watts, Inc., 730 Fifth Avenue, New York, N.Y. 10019.
Dance-a-Story: RCA Records—Educational Department, P.O. Box RCA 1000, Indianapolis, Ind. 46291.
Kaleidoscope: Programs for Children: Kaleidoscope, Box 284, Scituate, Mass. 02066.
Mother Goose Picture Sets: Hubbard Press, 2855 Shermer Road, Northbrook, Ill. 60062.
Tell and Draw Stories: Arts and Crafts Unlimited, P.O. Box 572, Minneapolis, Minn. 55440.

An interested mother watches her four-year-old son demonstrate creative use of brush and tempera in the library's improvised studio. Photo, taken at Franklin Lakes (N.J.) Free Public Library, courtesy The Record *(Hackensack, N.J.).*

PART 4

Parents in Search
of Information

Being a good parent requires a great deal of time—
time to talk with children, time to encourage them,
time to listen to them, time to respond to their emotions,
and time to work out all of the problems
children must face and eventually overcome.

Gerald M. Knox
"Six Ways to Help Your Child Learn More"
Better Homes and Gardens, April 1974, p. 34

Families in Reading

by Jane Granstrom

Three, a magic number in children's literature, is acquiring a new significance that reflects an exciting sharing of resources and experience among librarians, parents, and children. Library involvement in this tripartite relationship parallels the nationwide efforts of other educational, cultural, and recreational agencies to make the early years the cornerstone of each child's social and intellectual growth.

The early years are not a new library concern. The rhymes of Mother Goose were the earliest accepted standard books for preschoolers. Since the 1920s picture books, quite deliberately prepared and published for the young, have appeared with increasing frequency. *The Horn Book Magazine* began publication in 1924, and one of its goals was to acquaint booksellers, parents, and librarians with the very best books available for children. More recently (and now in its fourth edition) *A Parent's Guide to Children's Reading* has been published, explaining what to read and why. Most public libraries have supplied books of rhymes, picture books, magazines, and other publications aimed at parents. Children's librarians have always been eager to introduce these materials to parents who came to the library with their children. Many children's librarians, through the specialized format of the picture book hour, have been responsible for introducing young children to books. Recently, librarians—especially those involved in work with children—have more aggressively sought out the parent.

A number of reasons may account for the current focus on the early years. Funds are available for early childhood projects. Great numbers of young children must grow beyond the deprived areas in which they live. Producers

Jane Granstrom is Supervisor of Children's Services,
Thomas Crane Public Library, Quincy, Massachusetts.

Parents in Search of Information

of educational materials and services have discovered a ready market. Then, too, many mothers are seeking employment outside the home and must find day care for their preschoolers. This has led to an increasing number of jobs in the educational field—and to an increasing number of people directly concerned with the welfare of the very young.

But the most obvious reason for the current emphasis on this age group is our growing awareness that preschoolers can absorb basic knowledge and master the fundamentals of learning. Research has clearly established that an early start in the educative process leads to greater success in succeeding school years. Furthermore, early detection of special needs can lead to an individualized program of instruction that will enable the child to develop to his fullest potential.

Society's reaction to the needs of this age group has been remarkable. There has been a proliferation of private nursery schools and day care centers. Colleges and secondary schools offer programs in early childhood education. Elected officials have legislated for children's rights, for health programs, for programs to meet special needs. Television, food products, and toys have been the targets of justifiable criticism from individuals concerned with children's welfare. National efforts like Project Head Start and the Right to Read program are also outgrowths of this current interest in the early childhood years.

One must consider the impact of Project Head Start which, because it enriches a child's environment, has to involve the parent. Storytelling, the use of books, and visits to the library (as a community resource) are an intrinsic part of Head Start. This gives librarians an opportunity to reach parents through their children. Since Head Start staffers actively work with the parents of children from culturally-deprived neighborhoods, a certain level of receptivity for books, reading, and libraries is probably established among these parents.

The Right to Read program is another effort which recognizes parents as a vital force in the level of children's achievement. The purpose of this program is to eliminate the possibility of failure by mobilizing the resources of a community to establish a quality reading program. This goal is pursued in two ways: through work with the parents, especially the parents of preschoolers, to foster a child's readiness to learn; and, by meshing the school reading program with the public library program, to encourage those activities that support and supplement progress achieved in the school program.

Yet another book-oriented program recognizes the importance of parents, books, and libraries to children's academic achievement. Washington, D.C.'s Reading Is Fundamental program, initiated by Mrs. Robert McNamara, responded to the finding that most poor readers never had owned a book. RIF not only gave books to as many children and adults as possible but also stimulated greater use of libraries. Although RIF concentrates on school children

120

and not preschoolers, preschoolers benefit, too, because books used and shared in the home create an atmosphere for reading readiness.

School and public libraries have unique opportunities to promote children's reading through work with children and their parents. The special programs mentioned above offer chances to capitalize on parental involvement with children and books, chances that just shouldn't be missed.

Most parents of young children probably have not been exposed to preschool-level books for a considerable length of time, if ever. What can they expect? Toward what books will the librarian guide these parents? Picture books and other books that are easy to comprehend can be divided into numerous categories, but there are four major categories that provide a substantial framework for a librarian.

The majority of parents seek books that will give their children pleasure. Children readily enjoy the sound and meaning of words and the appearance and interpretive qualities of illustrations. Parents also seek "situation books" that fulfill a specific requirement of the parent. These books are used to introduce, explain, or familiarize a child with an event, state of being, or other situation. Information books are another category. Such books run the gamut from ABC's, to facts about animals, to how to make paper dolls. Many of these books have to be introduced to parents who may not have considered using information books with very young children. However, preschoolers enjoy these books since they deal with specific subject areas and can reinforce pleasurable experiences, such as a trip to the zoo or the arrival of a new pet.

The fourth category is the participation book. These books are enjoyable and actively involve the children. They may call for an immediate visual or verbal response, as in *Look Again* (Macmillan), when children guess the identity of something seen through a hole. The response may not come immediately; it may take as many as three readings before children join in on the infectious refrain in a book like *Millions of Cats* (Coward). Involvement may come after a book has been read and is being discussed. Many books are conducive to relaxed discussions that may heighten the enjoyment of the book when it is reread. An example of this type is *Rosie's Walk* (Macmillan), which stands by itself but is also fun to marvel at with children. When using a wordless book with young children, it is exciting to see the wide range of responses the children offer.

What have book-oriented parents come to expect from the library? A primary requisite has been a collection of books that their children will enjoy, a collection that includes rhymes, simple stories, perhaps alphabet and counting books. Secondly, parents would hope for a librarian who takes an interest in the children, who tries to learn more about the child with each visit and thereby tailor reading recommendations to that child. Finally, parents might hope for some very specific assistance, like suggestions for gift giving, the identification of a book recalled from childhood, or a substitute for the book that's become a day-in, day-out favorite. Such expectations are modest and realistic, and it's entirely possible that most parents will be completely satisfied if these simple needs are met. But these expectations fall short of what today's libraries can and should offer.

Not only must librarians vitalize service to book-oriented parents; they also must serve non-book-oriented parents. Libraries, limited as they are by finances and staff, must be more aggressive in order to reach the unreached. And libraries must be realistic in evaluating outreach efforts, recognizing that some people will never be attracted to libraries and reading, that some efforts are futile and some need modification. Each library must decide what outreach efforts are worth the attempt.

Some communities are willing to enclose printed matter from a town or city department in water or tax bills. Scout troops or friends of the library can cooperate on the composition, printing, and dissemination of materials to the home through the children. Librarians can bombard the local newspaper with varieties of articles; write to the woman's page; send items to the newsletters of churches, clubs, businesses; take advantage of public service announcements that local radio and television stations must broadcast. Cable television offers limitless opportunities.

Visibility outside libraries is also important—displays in community windows; fliers on community or supermarket bulletin boards. Picture book paperbacks deposited in the community health center or at the food stamp distribution center can have messages to parents pasted on the inside covers or can be placed with fliers of interest to parents. Parents could be reached by making library publications available in the offices of local obstetricians and pediatricians. There could even be a display of books with take-home materials in the maternity ward of the local hospital. If the hospital served an area encompassing several towns, the display could be maintained cooperatively. Libraries must experiment with all methods of saturation advertising.

Every year libraries are faced with an enormous outpouring of new picture books and easy-to-read publications. Such quantity means that librarians must be highly selective in their choices to offer a quality collection of adequate size. A good collection demands effort from the librarian in selecting it and in making broad use of each title. Availability of a particular book is enhanced by a librarian's ability to interpret that book to the public. The librarian must be completely familiar with the collection and recognize the multi-level nature of so many books. Most important is the desire to share this knowledge with the public. Ideally then, the librarian is actively serving the public by handling the books and interpreting them to parents and to children.

There are three major ways in which librarians serve both parents and children. Librarians serve children directly by providing books the children might enjoy. They serve children indirectly through their parents by providing books that parents feel their children need. Finally, they serve parents directly by providing books that broaden and deepen the parents' understanding of childhood. In the first two categories there will naturally be some overlapping. Hopefully, parents will continue to seek books for their children's enjoyment, and children will continue to feel free to express their needs to librarians. The most effective library service for this age group will be provided by those who are somewhat specialized in the literature for the early years and are familiar with materials for parents.

The pure enjoyment of books is one aspect that should not be relegated to a minor position, for it is the aspect with greatest appeal to the young reader. Children's book experiences move from the verbal to the visual/verbal as they grow older. They move, too, from books that must be shared to materials that can be enjoyed alone. Librarians are instrumental in this progression, initially guiding parents in the selection of simple rhymes and melodies, then introducing more complex narratives as the child grows older. Children also enjoy more complex illustrations as they grow older.

But librarians must be careful not to rely solely on chronology in recommending books. Parents who request books are frequently very specific in terms of age. They should have their requests met, but they should at the same time be led toward wider horizons. Many children have a high degree of awareness, are unusually perceptive, and have a fertile imagination that might go unnoticed in daily routines at home. When stimulated, these attributes make themselves known and contribute to the fullest development of the child's potential. Children are often willing to experiment with different kinds of books; it is the parents who must be won over. Librarians can talk to parents about a book and what it has to offer. Librarians can refer to what other children have said about specific books, what other parents have said, and what they themselves have gleaned from experience with the book in some library program. The range of books familiar to librarians enables them to recommend books similar to a child's favorites or different from those disliked. The burden of responsibility carried by librarians is lightened with the realization that the early enjoyment of books paves the way for reading readiness.

One of the objectives of Project Head Start was to supply children from deprived homes with experiences they would not get in the home environment. Such programmed experiences would bring the deprived child to an even level with the child from a more privileged home. These were basic experiences that Head Start hoped to provide, and they bore directly on children's future social and academic success. One of the methods used to supply these experiences was the sharing of books. "Sesame Street," offering vicarious experiences that provide for both social and intellectual growth, includes reading

Parents in Search of Information

aloud in its programming, has produced booklists, and even has its own books. So it can be seen that books are important to the developmental process.

Authors and publishers have capitalized on this experiential factor by producing books that deal very specifically with situations or conditions that children might encounter. These books—called "bibliotherapeutic" or "slice of life"—usually enable parents to cope with a particular situation. Such books, because they deal specifically with something a child views as negative, must be selected with the utmost care so that children who hear them read will have a positive experience. Books of this type frequently present behavioral patterns of childhood and can be used either as a cure or as a preventative. But at the very least they serve, in the hands of concerned parents, as an explanation, a softening of something that does disturb or could disturb a child. For instance, who wouldn't suggest *The Tenth Good Thing about Barney* (Atheneum) or *Nana Upstairs and Nana Downstairs* (Putnam) when parents request a book that would help them talk about death? Moving away, acceptance of a new baby, nightmares, are all topics that are called for and are being treated in picture books. Who wouldn't see that beside the pure enjoyment of Maurice Sendak's text and illustrations in *Where the Wild Things Are* (Harper & Row) and John Burmingham's *Mr. Gumpy's Outing* (Holt) these books offer some very positive emotional reinforcement for children? Bibliotherapy isn't original with the seventies, and neither is the need for it. But social conditions have altered so rapidly with the decade—divorce, lifestyles varying from the norm, working mothers, racially mixed marriages, the list is so long—that such books are needed not only by those children functioning within such a situation but also by children who must learn to be tolerant of lives different from their own.

Librarians working with children come to know the children's parents as parents, not just as adults. Such knowledge enables librarians to make available and recommend books on parenthood and childhood. Again, it's important that librarians become conversant with a spectrum of books published for adults about children—books that include such topics as children's rights, childhood diseases, the psychology of childhood, toys for children, and so forth. The children's librarian is naturally the person best able to promote such books. Many of these books can go hand in hand with picture books. For instance, the parent who looks for a book that will explain the doctor or the hospital to a very young child may also appreciate being shown a book on childhood diseases or a home medical encyclopedia. A picture book that explains death to a child can be paired with a book in the adult collection that suggests how parents can explain death to their children.

Books about children's books should not be relegated solely to children's librarians and students of children's literature. They, too, should be introduced to parents. Such books, with their combination of idealism and practicality, substantiate the case for using books with children, expand the adults' knowledge of what exists, give specific lists for specific ages, and explore such media as comics, inexpensive books for children, paperbacks, and gimmick books.

Research has proved not only that beginning the book habit at an early age increases the chances for educational success, but also that the children who develop a lifelong habit of reading are usually those accustomed to being read to, to seeing their parents read, to having reading materials in their home. Clearly then, it isn't enough simply to convince the child to borrow books; one must convince the parents to borrow books for themselves. This involves interdepartmental cooperation in public libraries and interagency cooperation between public and school libraries. Libraries are consumer hungry, too, and no opportunity to exploit the potential market should be overlooked.

The use of magazines with parents and children is one possible approach. Magazines as a form of literature vary in their quality, but they do offer reading matter, sources of information, pictorial material, and suggestions for activities. By introducing magazines to parents, the librarian is introducing a comparatively inexpensive source of reading material for the home. Since most magazines aim at a general age group, they have appeal for more than one family member, extending their usefulness.

The activities described in many magazines are related to arts and crafts, and as such offer an opportunity for shared experiences. Other recommended activities consist of games that can be played either individually or in a group. These, too, will require the attention of both children and parents. Some magazines, such as the *Sesame Street Magazine,* reinforce the concepts and information children are exposed to while watching television.

As ephemeral as we think the "ladies'" magazines are, they too are performing a very real service for children's books. Many December issues offer lists of gift books for children, compiled by such people as Nancy Larrick, editor, writer, and educator, and Gene Shalit, television critic and contributor to magazine and newspaper review columns. Lynda Johnson Robb edited an article, "Books They Loved," in the January 1969 issue of *McCalls* in which celebrities recalled their happiest childhood reading and stressed the importance of books in the home and reading aloud to children. Stories written and illustrated by noted children's authors and illustrators have also appeared in the holiday issues.

The librarian who is aware of such book lists and articles can capitalize on them with a lively news article or radio spot or by placing fliers where the magazines are sold. This kind of publicity could stress a "before you buy, borrow" approach, suggesting that people take advantage of library resources by examining titles recommended by non-librarians. Other sources of reviews are magazines like *Time, The Saturday Review, The New York Times Book*

Parents in Search of Information

Review, and *The Horn Book Magazine.* Again, an awareness of the titles reviewed or listed in these magazines provides opportunities to bring parents, children, and books together.

Librarians don't question the value of books in a child's life. They don't doubt that parents have a vital role in the development of reading habits among their children. Parents are natural resources, the first and most influential teachers of their children. How, then, are librarians going to draw children and their parents into the world of children's books?

The librarian can work with those parents who come to the library. Book lists and displays of both children's and adult titles can extend the interest of parents. A browsing collection could be available to parents who wait for their children during a film program or a picture book hour. A concurrent program for parents is also a means of involving parents in their children's book and library experiences.

In addition, libraries can sponsor programs just for parents dealing with aspects of parenthood and childhood, aspects that have their counterpart in the printed word. Libraries can promote more family programs at which they can demonstrate services and use of materials, distribute book lists, exhibit materials, and work with families in the selection of books and other media. Libraries are too often insular in their programming because most programs are offered in the libraries themselves. But every community has clubs and civic organizations that must offer programs to their membership. Libraries can volunteer to present or participate in those programs.

A suggested title might be: Families in Reading, and suggested topics for speeches might include:

Literature for the Preschooler (Genres, Themes, Styles)
Picture Book Art
Picture Book Hour (Why, How, With What, For Whom)
Books for Adults about Children
Library Materials for the Early Years
Gift Books for Young Children
Pre-Reading Materials
Books for the Beginning Reader
Building a Home Library
Early Childhood Projects and the Library
    The Right to Read
    Reading Is Fundamental
    Toy Library, etc.
Behavioral Patterns of Early Childhood and/or Bibliotherapy
Books about Children's Books
Magazines Parents Should Know About

Children, books, parents, and librarians—bringing them together and working toward the enrichment of childhood is a goal that will always be stimulating and challenging. There is no final answer because librarians are bound only by the limits of their own imaginations.

Bibliography

Arbuthnot, May Hill. *Children's Reading in the Home.* New York: Lothrop, Lee & Shepard, 1969.
   A helpful, well-annotated guide to books to read and share at home.
Chambers, Aiden. *Introducing Books to Children.* London: Heinemann Educational Books, 1973. (Copies of the publisher's edition are available from The Horn Book, Inc., Boston, Mass.).
Cianciolo, Patricia, ed. *Picture Books for Children.* Chicago: American Library Association, 1973.
   A bibliography of titles that will provide positive literature experiences, foster good reading habits, and promote the appreciation of graphic arts.
Foster, Joanna. *How to Conduct Effective Picture Book Programs.* White Plains, N.Y.: Westchester Library System, 1967.
   Sections on organizing, preparing, presenting, evaluating, and conducting a workshop.
Lanes, Selma. *Down the Rabbit Hole.* New York: Atheneum Publishers, 1971.
   A light and provocative examination of the "true" literature for early childhood.
Larrick, Nancy. *A Parent's Guide to Children's Reading.* rev. ed. Garden City, N.Y.: Doubleday & Co., 1975.
   A down-to-earth guide for the establishment of a lifetime habit of pleasure reading.
MacCann, Donnarae. *The Child's First Books.* Bronx, N.Y.: H. W. Wilson, 1973.
   An analysis of the literary and graphic elements in picture books for children from infancy to eight years.
Moore, Vardine. *Pre-School Story Hour.* Metuchen, N.J.: Scarecrow Press, 1972.
   A thorough, step-by-step guide to the purpose, planning, and production of story hours.
The RIF Handbook. Washington, D.C.: Reading Is Fundamental, 1973.
   A very complete handbook on how to organize an effective Reading Is Fundamental program in your community.
The Right to Read and the Nation's Libraries. Chicago: American Library Association, 1974.
   Reports from different sections of the country on Right to Read projects.

Libraries and Parent Education Programs

by Tommie M. Young

During the past century American families have experienced a series of changes that have led to alterations in family lifestyles, intra-family relations, value systems, and child-rearing practices. Families of today are nuclear in that each group of man, woman, and children forms an independent unit of its own, often far removed from relatives and friends known in childhood. Communities seem newer and less stable. All around are the symbols and voices of change, change, change.

Young parents, removed from the security of old and familiar family and friendship ties and lacking the reassurance of a stable community, want and need reinforcement, advice, and outlets for emotional pressures.

Some families, of course, may live close to relatives and childhood acquaintances. In times of stress these families have a network of sources upon which to call. But too often, when these families need and seek counsel and directions, the family and friendship web is incapable of giving help, or has information that the parents question or are reluctant to accept.

Still other families may be socially and professionally active, so busy outside the home that they have little time to give to their children. These fathers and mothers tend to lavish material objects on their children, while being awkward and embarrassed in implementing the intimate role of parent.

Changes in the family structure have meant an increase in the number of "one adult" homes. Such families are no longer always at the low end of the socio-economic scale, as more and more middle-class marriages are being dis-

Ms. Young is Director of Library Services, and Professor, North Carolina Agricultural and Technical State University, Greensboro, North Carolina.

solved. The case of the single parent adopting or taking on the responsibility of children is also more common.

Whatever the type of family—young, disadvantaged, socially active, solo-parent—the "family" in America needs aid and strengthening. Community and private agencies of many descriptions and purposes are needed to assist the family in achieving its goals and in helping each family member reach his or her fullest potential.

During the years 1971–72, North Carolina Central University School of Library Science undertook a unique project to aid American parents. Operating as a part of the Early Childhood Library Specialist Program, the parent program sought ways to reach parents not generally considered by library-oriented agencies.

A central objective of the parent program was to show parents how they could introduce their children to early and positive means of learning, discovering, and securing pleasures. By becoming more aware of their roles as parents and "teachers," mothers and fathers would realize that they could become "change agents" in the home by directing or redirecting the patterns and habits their children showed toward learning and leisure-time activities.

The program emerged as a three-faceted project including training in professional librarianship, a model early learning center, and the parent practicum. Parents in the program were mothers of the six four-year-old children selected as "practice subjects" for students undertaking practice work in the Early Learning Center.

Although the parent program was basically designed to provide practical experiences for the students involved in library science, it emerged as a program capable of functioning independently and addressed itself to the needs of parents of varied incomes, educational backgrounds, aspirations, and social status. Of the mothers enrolled in the program, the following descriptive labels could apply:

A. Young (under 35)
B. Above-average income
C. Below-average income
D. College educated
E. High school graduate
F. Less than high school
G. "Social climber"
H. Solo parent
I. Mature (over 35)
J. Two to five children
K. Over five children
L. One child

Parents in Search of Information

The following combinations were revealed:

1. ABDJ
2. CDHJ
3. CFK
4. BEIJ
5. BGIL
6. ACEHJ

Most frequent characteristics of the mothers were:

Young
Mature
Below average income
Below college education
Two or more children

The parent program began with a series of interviews. Having advertised the program in a variety of media, the students selected those parents who indicated a strong interest in participating in the routines associated with the program. These parents were invited to come in for an interview. Eventually six mothers were selected.

Program orientation included a one week practicum during which specialists in psychology, arts and crafts, learning theories, game play, and children's literature conducted daily workshops that encouraged parent participation. Observers (visiting educational leaders, administrators, and librarians) attended those sessions that interested them. The week's efforts were entitled "See How They Learn."

The practicums were a continuing activity and included quarterly evaluations and workshops that expanded the theme of the first week's conference. A good example of this expansion was seen in the summer practicum, "The Child's Literary Heritage: Folk and Fairy Literature." This activity involved three days devoted to exploring the cultural history of children's games, rhymes, and plays. Children and parents "experienced" a number of stories from many lands and compared the similarities in each. The "story experience," a term devised by the program director, was a standard format for storytelling. This phase draws on Frobelian concepts of using plays, games, and songs to emphasize a point, and incorporates activities generally associated with children's drama and motion education. It literally involves "lifting" a story from the pages of a book or the frame of a film and acting out the parts or dramatizing the scenes.

While each parent program may differ in its approach to particular topics, studies in the American family indicate several likely topic areas. Librarians themselves are aware of needs unique to the local community. The parent program format may include:

A. Orientation—During this phase of the program, background information is provided and the goals and purposes of the experience are defined.
B. Consideration of family topics—The program format, the length of each session, and the total length of the program must be determined by the program planners. Allow time to cover the following:
   1. An overview of child development
   2. The child's view of the parent
   3. How parents affect the child's emotional and intellectual development
   4. Role of the parent as a "change agent"
   5. Parents as role models for child's behavior
   6. Materials and activities for parents and children
   7. Selecting and implementing parent/child sharing time
      a. Things to do
      b. Places to go
      c. One-to-one interaction between parent and child
   8. Role of the library in community and family activities
C. Interim evaluations
D. Summary evaluation and follow-up

Parents maintained activity cards that were a record of the at home experiences in which the child and mother participated. These experiences were discussed during the quarterly practicum.

Perhaps the most revealing facts that came out of the parent program are:

Parents of diverse backgrounds can come together and share experiences that focus on their common interest in their children.

Parents, whatever their socio-economic status, are interested in helping their children and are willing to make sacrifices to do so if they are approached in a positive manner and can be shown the merits of their efforts.

Furthermore, libraries can initiate parent programs with relatively little money and enjoy reasonable success. The library as an ever-expanding service agency in the community is equally as prepared to offer parent programs as many other agencies.

Library agencies considering a parent program may be interested in these suggestions: The library staff, sensing a need in the local community, may initiate explorations aimed at determining the feasibility of the parent program idea. Librarians may find it desirable to collaborate with community

Parents in Search of Information

leaders and interested parents in most phases of planning and implementing a program. Persons that may be sought out for advice, counsel, and suggestions include childcare personnel, child development experts, physicians, and more parents.

The goals and objectives of a particular parent program will determine the amount of funds needed. Costs may vary from nearly nothing to quite a bit. To keep costs at a minimum, try cooperative ventures with other agencies, securing funds from private funding agencies, individual participation fees (a less desirable approach), and a wide use of volunteer assistance.

The most logical place to hold a library-related parent program is at the local library. Other possible locations include preschool centers, churches, public schools, community centers, lodges, or clubhouses. When selecting a site, consider accessibility of the quarters, ample and inviting space for meetings and discussions, and space for small group workshops. Electrical, safety, and sanitation facilities should also be of concern.

Insofar as possible, the library staff should comprise the core personnel. The staff can be supplemented by community personnel, including the parents themselves, health and social service personnel, artists, and so on.

Publicity for the program is vital to its success. Parents may be reached through the library, through agencies that serve young children—including nurseries, playschools, and day care centers—and through other children who attend the library or school.

Notices and announcements may be sent or presented to such organizations as PTA groups and civic and social groups. Publicity material may be placed in shopping centers and service areas of department stores, service stations, laundromats, and beauty and barber shops. Offices of social service agencies are good spots to place announcements. The news media are generally cooperative in such efforts. Radio, television, and newspapers should be contacted with information about the parent program.

The suggestions here have evolved from experience in launching a parent program. In a final word, the most important ingredients in undertaking such an effort are enthusiasm and a willingness to spend hours and hours in planning and implementing the project.

Bibliography

Cavan, Ruth S. *The American Family.* New York: Thomas Y. Crowell, 1969.

Hill, Reuben. *Families under Stress.* New York: Harper & Row, Publishers, Inc., 1949.

North Carolina Central University. School of Library Science. *Early Childhood Library Specialist Program.* Durham, N.C., 1971.

Ryan, Bernard, Jr. *Your Child and the First Year of School.* New York: World Publishing, 1969.

Prescribed for Preschool Problems

by Charlotte Leonard

The night was chilly and rainy as the bookmobile pulled up at the shopping center stop. A mother and her preschool boy were among the patrons waiting. As soon as the door opened, the preschooler asked, "Do you have *Mike Mulligan?*"

Luckily the book was in the picture book rack by the front door. The mother introduced herself to the librarian and said, "We have just moved here. We move around a lot. The first thing we do in a new city is go to the library and look for *Mike Mulligan.* As soon as we find him, Billy begins to feel at home."

Who says books cannot help when children have special problems? In this troubled world, many of the pressures adults feel are often felt to a lesser degree by preschoolers. They have numerous emotional adjustments to make and many new situations to face. Some of these problems will be explored in this article, along with suggestions of books which can help.

Getting Along within the Family

Very often one of the earliest emotional problems the preschooler faces is adjusting to a new baby in the family. The child no longer enjoys the parents' undivided attention; lots of time is spent on someone else. Visitors center their interest and affection on the new arrival. The crying and the demands the baby makes are annoying.

First of all, it is good to prepare the child as much as possible before the baby comes. *We Are Having a Baby* by Viki Holland does this through excellent black and white photographs. This book has proven to be a very successful gift from grandparents when their son's or daughter's family is expecting

Charlotte Leonard is Coordinator of Children's Services, Dayton and Montgomery County Public Library, Dayton, Ohio.

133

a second child. Some books approach the problem by suggesting to the child that growing up and out of the baby stage is a good experience. In *Peter's Chair* by Ezra Jack Keats, Peter discovers he has outgrown some of his possessions. When he finds this out, he does not mind giving them up to the new baby sister. Appealing to the child's sense of responsibility for the care of the new family member is the theme of Eloise Greenfield's *She Come Bringing Me That Little Baby Girl*. In *A Baby Sister for Frances* by Russell Hoban, the whole problem is seen through the eyes of a badger family.

Other members of the household, besides a new baby, can create tension. Older brothers and sisters are apt to be bossy; younger ones can be pesky and a nuisance to have around. Sometimes there is the feeling of rivalry or the pressure to be equal in talent or behavior. Psychologists have a lot to say about the middle child.

Books which present various relationships between brothers and sisters, both good and bad, can help the child understand his own frustrations and develop positive attitudes. Wendell, in *Send Wendell* by Genevieve Gray, is the victim of the whole family's imposition. He is always the one sent on errands. *The Day I Had to Play with My Sister* by Crosby Bonsall is a title that requires no explanation. The need to keep up with an older sister is the theme of *Almost Twins* by Dale Payson. *Tom in the Middle* by Berthe Amoss and *The One in the Middle Is the Green Kangaroo* by Judy Blume explore the position of the middle child.

Even getting along with mother and father can be a hassle. Parents sometimes do not understand, and they always have a lot of rules. Books that show there can be happy experiences between parents and children, along with inevitable disharmony, will give the child a sense of balance in day-to-day living. The title *And My Mean Old Mother Will Be Sorry, Blackboard Bear* by Martha Alexander expresses some of the preschooler's frustration in getting along with mother. On the other hand, *Rainy Day Together* by Ellen Parsons describes the companionship a mother and daughter experience when the weather is bad outside. *Friday Night Is Papa Night* by Ruth Sonneborn is a positive book about the excitement the whole family feels when father returns from working away all week.

What about grandparents? Maybe they are more of an answer to a problem than a problem. Little children soon discover that the slower pace of their grandparents, which parents mostly find annoying, is just right for them. They like not being hurried and covet the complete attention grandparents give. Children enjoy seeing experiences similar to theirs in books that show deep love, respect, and sometimes mutual dependence.

Two books, a little different from the usual kind about grandparents, are *Watch Out for the Chicken Feet in Your Soup* by Tomi De Paola, where a little boy introduces his grandmother to his friend, and *Kevin's Grandma* by Barbara Williams, in which two boys brag about their grandmothers. Ruth

Sonnenborn's *I Love Gram* tells of a little girl's concern when her grandmother is hospitalized. What it is like to become very old and forgetful is explored in *Matt's Grandfather* by Max Lundgren.

Not all families are neat and compact with fathers and mothers and grandparents all intact. There are many broken homes. Divorce is known to be a traumatic experience for husbands and wives, and this emotional upheaval is usually upsetting for the children as well. Knowing that other children go through similar separations and somehow adjust brings comfort and some sense of security.

In these trying situations, just having someone to listen may be important. This is the message Terry Berger gets across in *Friend Can Help. Emily and the Klunky Baby and the Next-Door Dog* by Joan Lexau would seem to be an unlikely title for a book concerned with separation, but when Daddy moves out, Emily decides to run away to find him. This book is full of deep emotional feelings. Another book by Joan Lexau, *Me Day,* expresses the idea that life can go on, relationships can be continued, and there can be happy times.

Adjusting to New Experiences

What happens when a family moves to a new neighborhood? For Billy, mentioned at the beginning of this article, there was a feeling of insecurity. For shy children and ones who have trouble making friends, it can be a lonely time. If the moving is from the city to the country, or the other way around, adjustments must be made. It may be that a best friend moves away, and the loss of a beloved playmate has to be endured. Perhaps, though, helping a new neighbor to feel at home might lessen the pain of losing a very good friend.

In *Who Will Be My Friends?* by Syd Hoff, Freddy likes his new home, his room, and his street. But the grown-ups do not have time for him and, at first, children his own age will not include him in their play. Shy Thomas finds dressing up as a tiger on Halloween gives him courage to get acquainted in his new neighborhood, in *A Tiger Called Thomas* by Charlotte Zolotow. In another book by the same author, *Janey* is the best friend who moves away, and the lonely little girl who misses her dreams of their living next door again when they grow up. For Kathy who moves from the country to the city, it is a *Sad Day Glad Day* as she leaves behind her flowers, apple tree, and swing in the book by Vivian Thompson. Nancy in *Noisy Nancy and Nick* by LouAnn Gaeddert reaches out and helps her new neighbor to feel at home.

Even if one never moves, the whole problem of making and keeping friends is a continuing one for all ages. Developing friendships requires patience, give and take, and selectivity. Through books little children can learn what a friend is, that making friends is something one has to work at, that liking the same things can be the beginning of friendship, and that friends are not always perfect.

What is a friend? *A Friend Is Someone Who Likes You* says Joan Walsh

Parents in Search of Information

Anglund. That it is nice to have *Best Friends* is the message from Miriam Cohen. Maybe the best friend will be *My Friend John* described by Charlotte Zolotow. John knows all of his friend's likes and dislikes and accepts him as he is. In the story by Mary Lystad, George discovers that he and *That New Boy* have something in common—they both like animals. When one child acts bossy and the other becomes angry, conflict results in *Let's Be Enemies* by Janice Udry. But friendship can warm a cold day when one little girl says to another *Hold My Hand* by Charlotte Zolotow.

Going to school, either nursery school or kindergarten, is probably the first really big experience for the child out on his or her own. Being placed in a totally new environment, separated from mother and transplanted into the midst of a large group of strange children, makes for three big adjustments. Prior to going to school, the child will ask many questions: What goes on in school? Will I be able to do it? Will the teacher be nice? Will the other children like me? Insecurity, fear, and lack of confidence may all be a part of the child's first feelings.

Some books will prepare the child for what to expect. Several that do this are *First Day in School* by Bill Binzen, *Shawn Goes to School* by Petronella Breinburg, and *Come with Me to Nursery School* by Edith Hurd. The experience of saying goodbye to mother is explored in *Goodbye, Hello* by Robert Welber. Some of the child's apprehension of relating to the teacher is treated in *The New Teacher* by Miriam Cohen. In another book by the same author, there is an answer to the question *Will I Have a Friend?*

One experience all preschoolers share is that of being ill. Feeling sick is no fun, and children need understanding, sympathy, and special attention at this time. When this experience involves doctors and hospitals, the fear of the unknown is great. Preparing the child for what a doctor may do and giving some information about what to expect during a hospital stay will make that first visit to the doctor's office or the hospital an interesting experience rather than a frightening one.

A very reassuring book that pursues the idea that being just a little sick can be a nice change of pace is *A Day Off* by Tobi Tobias. In *Just Awful* by Alma Whitney, a cut finger sends six-year-old James to the school nurse. After getting a bandage and a hug, James returns to class to tell his teacher, "I think I'm going to be all right." Some books that describe going to the doctor and to the hospital are *My Doctor* by Harlow Rockwell; *Nicky Goes to the Doctor* by Richard Scarry; *Jeff's Hospital Book* by Harriet Sobol; and *Elizabeth Gets Well* by Alfons Weber. These books contain just enough interesting information for the preschooler to absorb and will satisfy curiosity and allay fears.

Certainly at some point in the preschool years, the child will experience the death of a pet. Usually this is a dog, less frequently a cat or a bird. In addition to the tears that follow and the extended weeks of grief, there will be the confused feeling about death and what it means. The child may also experience the death of a grandparent or even some other member of the family. How can the child be comforted? What can be said to give meaning to this complex subject?

Sandol Warburg's *Growing Time* deals with the death of a boy's pet dog and his grandmother's understanding that there needs to be a period to grieve. *The Tenth Good Thing about Barney* by Judith Viorst is about a family of children and the eulogy they write for the funeral service held for their beloved cat. In *Annie and the Old One* by Miska Miles, the Indian grandmother is about to die. She says that she will only last until after the rug is finished on the loom. Annie hopes to prevent death by unravelling the work each day. When she is discovered, she learns from her grandmother not only about death but about life as well.

Growing Up

People never really finish growing up; the maturing process goes on and on. Little children grow a step at a time. Getting over being afraid of the dark is one step. All sorts of imaginary animals and monsters mysteriously appear at night. Much reassurance is needed to make bedtime a winding down time, a time to be enjoyed instead of dreaded.

Lullabies and soothing stories are recommended for the going-to-bed ritual. A relaxing picture book, *All the Pretty Horses* by Susan Jeffers, is based on a lullaby. Some books which present night experiences in a positive manner are: *A Child's Good Night Book* and *Goodnight Moon* by Margaret Wise Brown, *Night's Nice* by Barbara and Ed Emberley, and *The Moon Jumpers* by Janice Udry. These are all calm and quiet picture books that will help reinforce good feelings about the night. Facing up to the problem of nighttime monsters wandering about are such titles as: *The Something* by Natalie Babbitt, *10 Bears in My Bed—A Goodnight Countdown* by Stan Mack, *There's a Nightmare in My Closet* by Mercer Mayer, and *The Alligator under the Bed* by Joan Nixon. These stories are more funny than scary, and they let children know that other children have imaginations similar to theirs.

Learning to show affection is another part of the maturing process. Little children can begin to do this through caring for their dolls and teddy bears. Sometimes the objects of their affections also provide a feeling of security. Preschoolers should be encouraged to reach out beyond themselves in their play experiences.

Boys need not be ashamed to show affection and love. A grandmother understands this and buys William a doll in the book *William's Doll* by Charlotte Zolotow. When *Ira Sleeps Over* in a book by Bernard Waber, Ira discovers his friend loves his teddy bear as much as he does. Lisa takes all of her money from her piggy bank to buy *Corduroy*, by Don Freeman. *Mommy,*

Parents in Search of Information

Buy Me a China Doll is the plea in the folksong written and pictured by Harve and Margot Zemach. *I'll Protect You from the Jungle Beasts* is the promise a little boy makes to his teddy bear, but the teddy bear ends up protecting him in the story by Martha Alexander.

Fitting into acceptable behavior patterns is not only a daily challenge for preschoolers but also a big problem for society as a whole. The jails are full, many city streets are unsafe, and whole nations have difficulty living in peace. With little children, there will be frequent disobedience, willfulness, displays of temper, grumpiness, and meanness. Reading aloud to discover other children's experiences will offer a springboard for family counseling sessions.

One of the favorite books of children is Maurice Sendak's *Where the Wild Things Are,* in which young Max misbehaves to such a degree that his mother calls him a "wild thing." Following his deserved punishment, the book ends with his mother showing she loves him after all. All children can relate to this experience. The classic *Tale of Peter Rabbit* by Beatrix Potter has kept its appeal through the years because disobedient Peter is so real and understandable. But girls can be just as naughty, too. No one dreams that sweet little Tulip is the mean one in the story about two raccoons, *Benjamin and Tulip* by Rosemary Wells, but she gets her comeuppance in the end. *Did You Ever Hear a Klunk Say Please?* The Klunk children, in the book by Leonard Kessler, do not like to wash, they gulp down their food, fight at play, disobey signs, and leave their toys scattered about. Selfishness, frequently the cause of bad behavior, is explored in a number of books. Robert Kraus's character, *Rebecca Hatpin,* always thinks of herself first until the flu epidemic invades the neighborhood, and she discovers that helping others can be fun. *I Do Not Like It When My Friend Comes to Visit* by Ivan Sherman describes a little girl's frustrations with sharing her toys. *Sometimes I'm Jealous* by Jane Watson and *I Was So Mad!* by Norma Simon explore negative feelings.

Learning to know oneself, assessing one's capabilities and weaknesses, and developing self-identity are all necessary for adult mental health. Preschoolers have similar needs. They need to understand themselves and feel a sense of independence and achievement.

The women's liberation movement has encouraged the publication of such books as *Girls Can Be Anything* by Norma Klein and *Boys & Girls, Girls & Boys* by Eve Merriam. In the story, *Who Are You Today?* by Richard Shaw, Jeff pretends to be lots of different people before he ends up saying, "Mom, starting today, I think I'll be ME." The heroine in *Someday* by Charlotte Zolotow dreams of the time when everything she does will be perfect. Evan, in *Evan's Corner* by Elizabeth Hill, realizes that he needs privacy in order to be himself.

Closely allied with the building of self-identity is the development of personal interests. A lively curiosity and healthy imagination can help the child's personality to take shape.

Prescribed for Preschool Problems

Maurice's Room by Paula Fox and *The Awful Mess* by Ann Rockwell may not be examples of good housekeeping, but both stories introduce boys with lots of interests. Channeling imagination in the right direction can spark the development of a creative mind. Fun titles in this area are *My Mama Says There Aren't Any Zombies, Ghosts, Vampires, Creatures, Demons, Monsters, Fiends, Goblins, or Things* by Judith Viorst, *And To Think That I Saw It on Mulberry Street* by Dr. Seuss, and *Sam, Bangs, and Moonshine* by Evaline Ness.

The conclusion to be drawn from all of this is that little children have a number of important emotional adjustments to make and that there are many appropriate books which speak to their specific problems. Parents, grandparents, teachers, nurses, other hospital personnel, and Sunday school teachers can find additional material in the entertaining stories listed at the end of this article.

Books Relating to Behavior and Feelings

GETTING ALONG WITHIN THE FAMILY

Accepting New Babies

Alexander, Martha. *Nobody Asked Me If I Wanted a Baby Sister.* Illus. by the author. New York: Dial Press, 1971.

Bell, Gina. *Who Wants Willy Wells?* Illus. by Jean Tamburine. Nashville: Abingdon Press, 1965.

Berenstain, Stanley. *Berenstain Bears' New Baby.* Illus. by the author. New York: Random House, Inc., 1974.

Berger, Terry. *New Baby.* Photographs by Heinz Kluetmeier. Chicago: Childrens Press, 1974.

Borack, Barbara. *Someone Small.* Illus. by Anita Lobel. New York: Harper & Row Publishers, Inc., 1969.

Byars, Betsy. *Go and Hush the Baby.* Illus. by Emily McCully. New York: Viking Press, 1971.

Chandler, Edna. *Five Cent, Five Cent.* Illus. by Betty Stull. Chicago: Albert Whitman & Co., 1967.

Greenfield, Eloise. *She Come Bringing Me That Little Baby Girl.* Illus. by John Steptoe. Philadelphia: J. B. Lippincott Co., 1974.

Hoban, Russell. *A Baby Sister for Frances.* Illus. by Lillian Hoban. New York: Harper & Row Publishers, Inc., 1964.

Holland, Viki. *We Are Having a Baby.* Photographs by the author. New York: Charles Scribner's Sons, 1972.

Jarrell, Mary. *The Knee-Baby.* Illus. by Symeon Shimin. New York: Farrar, Straus and Giroux, Inc., 1973.

Keats, Ezra Jack. *Peter's Chair.* Illus. by the author. New York: Harper & Row Publishers, Inc., 1967.

Parents in Search of Information

Mann, Peggy. *That New Baby.* Illus. by Susanne Suba. New York: Coward, McCann & Geoghegan, 1967.

Schick, Eleanor. *Peggy's New Brother.* Illus. by the author. New York: Macmillan Publishing Co., 1970.

Fitting In with Brothers and Sisters

Amoss, Berthe. *Tom in the Middle.* Illus. by the author. New York: Harper & Row Publishers, Inc., 1968.

Berger, Terry. *Big Sister, Little Brother.* Photographs by Heinz Kluetmeier. Chicago: Childrens Press, 1974.

Blume, Judy. *The One in the Middle Is the Green Kangaroo.* Illus. by Lois Axeman. Chicago: Reilly & Lee, 1969.

Bonsall, Crosby. *The Day I Had to Play with My Sister.* Illus. by the author. New York: Harper & Row Publishers, Inc., 1972.

———. *Piggle.* Illus. by the author. New York: Harper & Row Publishers, Inc., 1973.

Chenery, Janet. *Wolfie.* Illus. by Marc Simont. New York: Harper & Row Publishers, Inc., 1969.

Conta, Marcia. *Feelings between Brothers and Sisters.* Photographs by Jules M. Rosenthal. Chicago: Childrens Press, 1974.

Ellentuck, Shan. *My Brother Bernard.* Illus. by the author. New York: Abelard-Schuman, Ltd., 1968.

Gray, Genevieve S. *Send Wendell.* Illus. by Symeon Shimin. New York: McGraw-Hill Book Co., 1974.

Hoban, Russell. *A Birthday for Frances.* Illus. by Lillian Hoban. New York: Harper & Row Publishers, Inc., 1968.

Hutchins, Pat. *Titch.* Illus. by the author. New York: Macmillan Publishing Co., 1971.

Lasker, Joe. *He's My Brother.* Illus. by the author. Chicago: Albert Whitman & Co., 1974.

Ness, Evaline. *Exactly Alike.* Illus. by the author. New York: Charles Scribner's Sons, 1964.

Ormondroyd, Edward. *Theodore's Rival.* Illus. by John Larrecq. Berkeley: Parnassus Press, 1971.

Payson, Dale. *Almost Twins.* Illus. by the author. Englewood Cliffs, N.J.: Prentice-Hall, Inc., 1974.

Scott, Ann. *Sam.* Illus. by Symeon Shimin. New York: McGraw-Hill Book Co., 1967.

Viorst, Judith. *I'll Fix Anthony.* Illus. by Arnold Lobel. New York: Harper & Row Publishers, Inc., 1969.

Wells, Rosemary. *Noisy Nora.* Illus. by the author. New York: Dial Press, 1973.

Zolotow, Charlotte. *Big Sister and Little Sister.* Illus. by Martha Alexander. New York: Harper & Row Publishers, Inc., 1966.

———. *Do You Know What I'll Do?* Illus. by Garth Williams. New York: Harper & Row Publishers, Inc., 1958.

———. *If It Weren't for You.* Illus. by Ben Shecter. New York: Harper & Row Publishers, Inc., 1966.

Appreciating Grandparents

Borack, Barbara. *Grandpa.* Illus. by Ben Shecter. New York: Harper & Row Publishers, Inc., 1967.

Buckley, Helen. *Grandfather and I.* Illus. by Paul Galdone. New York: Lothrop, Lee & Shepard, 1959.

———. *Grandmother and I.* Illus. by Paul Galdone. New York: Lothrop, Lee & Shepard, 1959.

De Paola, Tomi. *Watch Out for the Chicken Feet in Your Soup.* Illus. by the author. Englewood Cliffs, N.J.: Prentice-Hall, Inc., 1974.

Gauch, Patricia. *Grandpa and Me.* Illus. by Symeon Shimin. New York: Coward, McCann & Geoghegan, 1972.

Lexau, Joan. *Benjie.* Illus. by Don Bolognese. New York: Dial Press, 1964.

———. *Benjie on His Own.* Illus. by Don Bolognese. New York: Dial Press, 1970.

Lundgren, Max. *Matt's Grandfather.* Illus. by Fibben Hald. New York: G. P. Putnam's Sons, 1972.

Minarik, Else. *Little Bear's Visit.* Illus. by Maurice Sendak. New York: Harper & Row Publishers, Inc., 1961.

Sonneborn, Ruth A. *I Love Gram.* Illus. by Leo Carty. New York: Viking Press, 1971.

Williams, Barbara. *Kevin's Grandma.* Illus. by Kay Chorao. New York: E. P. Dutton & Co., Inc., 1975.

Understanding Parents

Alexander, Martha. *And My Mean Old Mother Will Be Sorry, Blackboard Bear.* Illus. by the author. New York: Dial Press, 1972.

Brown, Margaret Wise. *The Runaway Bunny.* Illus. by Clement Hurd. New York: Harper & Row Publishers, Inc., 1942.

Conta, Marcia. *Feelings between Kids and Parents.* Photographs by Jules M. Rosenthal. Chicago: Childrens Press, 1974.

Fisher, Aileen. *Do Bears Have Mothers, Too?* Illus. by Eric Carle. New York: Thomas Y. Crowell Co., 1973.

———. *In the Middle of the Night.* Illus. by Adrienne Adams. New York: Thomas Y. Crowell Co., 1965.

Parents in Search of Information

———. *My Mother and I.* Illus. by Kazue Mizumura. New York: Thomas Y. Crowell Co., 1967.

Flack, Marjorie. *Ask Mr. Bear.* Illus. by the author. New York: Macmillan Publishing Co., 1932.

Minarik, Else. *Little Bear.* Illus. by Maurice Sendak. New York: Harper & Row Publishers, Inc., 1957.

Mizumura, Kazue. *If I Were a Mother . . .* Illus. by the author. New York: Thomas Y. Crowell Co., 1968.

Monjo, F. N. *The One Bad Thing about Father.* Illus. by Rocco Negri. New York: Harper & Row Publishers, Inc., 1971.

Parsons, Ellen. *Rainy Day Together.* Illus. by Lillian Hoban. New York: Harper & Row Publishers, Inc., 1971.

Sharmat, Marjorie. *I Want Mama.* Illus. by Emily McCully. New York: Harper & Row Publishers, Inc., 1974.

Sonneborn, Ruth. *Friday Night Is Papa Night.* Illus. by Ben Shecter. New York: Harper & Row Publishers, Inc., 1971.

Stanek, Muriel. *My Family and I.* Illus. by Jean W. Morey. Westchester, Ill.: Benefic Press, 1967.

Stewart, Robert. *The Daddy Book.* Illus. by Don Madden. New York: American Heritage Press, 1972.

Stover, Jo Ann. *I'm in a Family.* Illus. by the author. New York: David McKay Co., Inc., 1966.

Thayer, June. *Andy and the Wild Worm.* Illus. by Beatrice Darwin. New York: William Morrow & Co., Inc., 1973.

Udry, Janice. *What Mary Jo Shared.* Illus. by Eleanor Mill. Chicago: Albert Whitman & Co., 1966.

Young, Miriam. *Peas in a Pod.* Illus. by Linda Neely. New York: G. P. Putnam's Sons, 1971.

Zolotow, Charlotte. *Mr. Rabbit and the Lovely Present.* Illus. by Maurice Sendak. New York: Harper & Row Publishers, Inc., 1962.

———. *When I Have a Son.* Illus. by Hilary Knight. New York: Harper & Row Publishers, Inc., 1967.

Learning about Adoption

Caines, Jeannette. *Abby.* Illus. by Steven Kellogg. New York: Harper & Row Publishers, Inc., 1973.

Wasson, Valentina Pavlovna. *The Chosen Baby.* Illus. by Hildegarde Woodward. Philadelphia: J. B. Lippincott Co., 1950.

Coping with Divorce

Berger, Terry. *Friend Can Help.* Photographs by Heinz Kluetmeier. Chicago: Childrens Press, 1974.

Goff, Beth. *Where Is Daddy?* Illus. by Susan Perl. New York: Beacon Press, 1960.

Lexau, Joan. *Emily and the Klunky Baby and the Next-Door Dog.* Illus. by Martha Alexander. New York: Dial Press, 1972.

———. *Me Day.* Illus. by Robert Weaver. New York: Dial Press, 1971.

Zolotow, Charlotte. *A Father like That.* Illus. by Ben Shecter. New York: Harper & Row Publishers, Inc., 1971.

ADJUSTING TO NEW EXPERIENCES

Moving Away

Baldwin, Anne. *A Friend in the Park.* Illus. by Ati Forberg. New York: Four Winds Press, 1973.

Brown, Myra. *Pip Moves Away.* Illus. by Polly Jackson. Los Angeles: Golden Gate Junior Books, 1967.

Felt, Sue. *Hello, Goodbye.* Illus. by the author. New York: Doubleday & Co., 1960.

Gaeddert, LouAnn. *Noisy Nancy and Nick.* Illus. by Gioia Fiammenghi. New York: Doubleday & Co., 1970.

———. *Too Many Girls.* Illus. by Marilyn Hafner. New York: Coward, McCann & Geoghegan, 1972.

Hoff, Syd. *Who Will Be My Friends?* Illus. by the author. New York: Harper & Row Publishers, Inc., 1960.

Kantrowitz, Mildred. *Good-bye, Kitchen.* Illus. by Mercer Mayer. New York: Parents' Magazine Press, 1972.

Thompson, Vivian. *Sad Day, Glad Day.* Illus. by Lillian Obligado. New York: Holiday House, Inc., 1962.

Zolotow, Charlotte. *Janey.* Illus. by Ronald Himler. New York: Harper & Row Publishers, Inc., 1973.

———. *A Tiger Called Thomas.* Illus. by Kurt Werth. New York: Lothrop, Lee & Shepard, 1963.

Making and Keeping Friends

Alexander, Martha. *Blackboard Bear.* Illus. by the author. New York: Dial Press, 1969.

Anglund, Joan Walsh. *A Friend Is Someone Who Likes You.* Illus. by the author. New York: Harcourt Brace Jovanovich, Inc., 1958.

Beim, Lorraine. *Two Is a Team.* Illus. by Ernest Crichlow. New York: Harcourt Brace Jovanovich, Inc., 1945.

Berger, Terry. *Being Alone, Being Together.* Photographs by Heinz Kluetmeier. Chicago: Childrens Press, 1974.

Cohen, Miriam. *Best Friends.* Illus. by Lillian Hoban. New York: Macmillan Publishing Co., 1971.

Parents in Search of Information

Conta, Marcia. *Feelings between Friends.* Photographs by Jules M. Rosenthal. Chicago: Childrens Press, 1974.

Craig, M. Jean. *The New Boy on the Sidewalk.* Illus. by Sheila Greenwald. New York: W. W. Norton & Co., 1967.

DeRegniers, Beatrice. *May I Bring a Friend?* Illus. by Beni Montresor. New York: Atheneum Publishers, 1964.

Kafka, Sherry. *I Need a Friend.* Illus. by Eros Keith. New York: G. P. Putnam's Sons, 1971.

Keats, Ezra Jack. *A Letter to Amy.* Illus. by the author. New York: Harper & Row Publishers, Inc., 1968.

Krasilovsky, Phyllis. *The Shy Little Girl.* Illus. by Trina Schart Hyman. Boston: Houghton Mifflin Co., 1970.

Lystad, Mary H. *That New Boy.* Illus. by Emily McCully. New York: Crown Publishers, 1973.

McGovern, Ann. *Scram, Kid!* Illus. by Nola Langner. New York: Viking Press, 1974.

Minarik, Else. *Little Bear's Friend.* Illus. by Maurice Sendak. New York: Harper & Row Publishers, Inc., 1960.

Sharmat, Marjorie. *Sophie and Gussie.* New York: Macmillan Publishing Co., 1973.

Viorst, Judith. *Rosie and Michael.* Illus. by Lorna Tomei. New York: Atheneum Publishers, 1974.

Waber, Bernard. *Nobody Is Perfick.* Illus. by the author. Boston: Houghton Mifflin, 1971.

Wiseman, Bernard. *Little New Kangaroo.* Illus. by Robert Lopshire. New York: Macmillan Publishing Co., 1973.

Yashima, Taro. *Youngest One.* Illus. by the author. New York: Viking Press, 1962.

Zolotow, Charlotte. *The Hating Book.* Illus. by Ben Shecter. New York: Harper & Row Publishers, Inc., 1969.

———. *Hold My Hand.* Illus. by Thomas di Grazia. New York: Harper & Row Publishers, Inc., 1972.

———. *My Friend John.* Illus. by Ben Shecter. New York: Harper & Row Publishers, Inc., 1968.

———. *The Unfriendly Book.* Illus. by William Pene Du Bois. New York: Harper & Row Publishers, Inc., 1975.

Going to School

Babbitt, Lorraine. *Pink like the Geranium.* Illus. by Arnold Dobrin. Chicago: Childrens Press, 1973.

Binzen, Bill. *First Day in School.* Illus. by the author. New York: Doubleday Publishing Co., 1972.

Breinburg, Petronella. *Shawn Goes to School.* Illus. by Errol Lloyd. New York: Thomas Y. Crowell Co., 1973.

Caudill, Rebecca. *Did You Carry the Flag Today, Charley?* Illus. by Nancy Grossman. New York: Holt, Rinehart & Winston, 1966.

———. *Pocketful of Cricket.* Illus. by Evaline Ness. New York: Holt, Rinehart & Winston, 1964.

Cohen, Miriam. *The New Teacher.* Illus. by Lillian Hoban. New York: Macmillan Publishing Co., 1967.

Haas, Dorothy. *A Special Place for Jonny.* Illus. by David K. Stone. Racine, Wis.: Whitman Publishing Co., 1966.

Hurd, Edith. *Come with Me to Nursery School.* Photographs by Edward Bigelow. New York: Coward, McCann & Geoghegan, 1970.

Levy, Elizabeth. *Nice Little Girls.* Illus. by Mordecai Gerstein. New York: Delacorte Press, 1974.

Mannheim, Grete. *The Two Friends.* Illus. by the author. New York: Alfred A. Knopf, Inc., 1968.

Welber, Robert. *Goodbye, Hello.* Illus. by Cyndy Szekeres. New York: Pantheon Books, 1974.

Learning about Illness, Hospitals, and Doctors

Bemelmans, Ludwig. *Madeline.* Illus. by the author. New York: Viking Press, 1939.

Breinburg, Petronella. *Doctor Shawn.* Illus. by Errol Lloyd. New York: Thomas Y. Crowell Co., 1974.

Hurd, Edith. *Johnny Lion's Bad Day.* Illus. by Clement Hurd. New York: Harper & Row Publishers, Inc., 1970.

Raskin, Ellen. *Spectacles.* Illus. by the author. New York: Atheneum Publishers, 1972.

Rockwell, Harlow. *My Doctor.* Illus. by the author. New York: Macmillan Publishing Co., 1973.

Scarry, Richard. *Nicky Goes to the Doctor.* Illus. by the author. Racine, Wis.: Golden Press, 1971.

Sobol, Harriet L. *Jeff's Hospital Book.* Photographs by Patricia Agre. New York: Henry Z. Walck, Inc., 1975.

Tobias, Tobi. *A Day Off.* Illus. by Ray Cruz. New York: G. P. Putnam's Sons, 1973.

Weber, Alfons. *Elizabeth Gets Well.* Illus. by Jacqueline Blass. New York: Thomas Y. Crowell Co., 1970.

Whitney, Alma M. *Just Awful.* Illus. by Lillian Hoban. Reading, Mass.: Addison-Wesley Publishing Co., 1971.

Williams, Barbara. *Albert's Toothache.* Illus. by Kay Chorao. New York: E. P. Dutton & Co., Inc., 1974.

Parents in Search of Information

Wolff, Angelika. *Mom! I Broke My Arm!* Illus. by Leo Glueckselig. New York: Lion Press, Inc., 1969.

———. *Mom! I Need Glasses!* Illus. by Dorothy Hill. New York: Lion Press, Inc., 1970.

Understanding Death

Abbott, Sarah. *The Old Dog.* Illus. by George Mocniak. New York: Coward, McCann & Geoghegan, 1972.

Brown, Margaret Wise. *The Dead Bird.* Illus. by Remy Charlip. Reading, Mass.: William R. Scott, Inc., 1958.

De Paola, Tomi. *Nana Upstairs & Nana Downstairs.* Illus. by the author. New York: G. P. Putnam's Sons, 1973.

Harris, Audrey. *Why Did He Die?* Illus. by Susan Dalke. Minneapolis: Lerner Publications, 1965.

Miles, Miska. *Annie and the Old One.* Illus. by Peter Parnall. Boston: Little, Brown & Co., 1971.

Viorst, Judith. *The Tenth Good Thing about Barney.* Illus. by Erik Blegvad. New York: Atheneum Publishers, 1971.

Warburg, Sandol. *Growing Time.* Illus. by Leonard Weisgard. Boston: Houghton Mifflin, 1969.

Zolotow, Charlotte. *My Grandson Lew.* Illus. by William Pene du Bois. New York: Harper & Row Publishers, Inc., 1974.

GROWING UP

Overcoming Fears

Babbitt, Natalie. *The Something.* Illus. by the author. New York: Farrar, Straus, & Giroux, Inc., 1970.

Beckman, Per and Kaj. *Lisa Cannot Sleep.* Illus. by the authors. New York: Franklin Watts, Inc., 1970.

Bradbury, Ray. *Switch on the Night.* Illus. by Madeline Gekiere. New York: Pantheon Books, 1955.

Brown, Margaret Wise. *A Child's Good Night Book.* Illus. by the author. Reading, Mass.: William R. Scott, Inc., 1950.

———. *Goodnight Moon.* Illus. by Clement Hurd. New York: Harper & Row Publishers, Inc., 1947.

Buckley, Helen E. *Michael Is Brave.* Illus. by Emily McCully. New York: Lothrop, Lee & Shepard Co., 1971.

Clifton, Lucille. *Good, Says Jerome.* Illus. by Stephanie Douglas. New York: E. P. Dutton & Co., 1973.

Coatsworth, Elizabeth. *Good Night.* Illus. by Jose Aruego. New York: Macmillan Publishing Co., 1972.

Cole, William. *Frances Face-Maker.* Illus. by Tomi Ungerer. New York: Collins-World Publishing Co., Inc., 1963.

De Paola, Tomi. *Fight the Night.* Illus. by the author. Philadelphia: J. B. Lippincott Co., 1968.

Emberley, Barbara and Ed. *Night's Nice.* Illus. by Ed Emberley. New York: Doubleday Publishing Co., 1963.

Hazen, Barbara Shook. *Where Do Bears Sleep?* Illus. by Ian E. Staunton. Reading, Mass.: Addison-Wesley Publishing Co., 1970.

Hoban, Russell. *Bedtime for Frances.* Illus. by Garth Williams. New York: Harper & Row Publishers, Inc., 1960.

Jeffers, Susan. *All the Pretty Horses.* Illus. by the author. New York: Macmillan Publishing Co., 1974.

Keats, Ezra Jack. *Dreams.* Illus. by the author. New York: Macmillan Publishing Co., 1974.

Lifton, Betty Jean. *Good Night Orange Monster.* Illus. by Cyndy Szekeres. New York: Atheneum Publishers, 1972.

Litchfield, Ada. *The Good Night Sleep Tight Book.* Illus. by Ruth Hartshorn. Austin, Texas: Steck-Vaughn Co., 1969.

Mack, Stan. *10 Bears in My Bed–A Goodnight Countdown.* Illus. by the author. New York: Pantheon Books, 1974.

Mayer, Mercer. *There's a Nightmare in My Closet.* Illus. by the author. New York: Dial Press, 1968.

———. *You're the Scaredy-Cat.* Illus. by the author. New York: Parents' Magazine Press, 1974.

Nixon, Joan. *The Alligator under the Bed.* Illus. by Jan Hughes. New York: G. P. Putnam's Sons, 1974.

Ryan, Cheli. *Hildilid's Night.* Illus. by Arnold Lobel. New York: Macmillan Publishing Co., 1971.

Showers, Paul. *Sleep Is for Everyone.* Illus. by Wendy Watson. New York: Thomas Y. Crowell Co., 1974.

Udry, Janice. *The Moon Jumpers.* Illus. by Maurice Sendak. New York: Harper & Row Publishers, Inc., 1959.

Zolotow, Charlotte. *Summer Night.* Illus. by Ben Shecter. New York: Harper & Row Publishers, Inc., 1974.

Learning to Show Affection

Alexander, Martha. *I'll Protect You from the Jungle Beasts.* Illus. by the author. New York: Dial Press, 1973.

Caudill, Rebecca. *The Best-Loved Doll.* Illus. by Elliott Gilbert. New York: Holt, Rinehart & Winston, 1962.

Freeman, Don. *Corduroy.* Illus. by the author. New York: Viking Press, 1968.

Hoban, Lillian. *Arthur's Honey Bear.* Illus. by the author. New York: Harper & Row Publishers, Inc., 1974.

Parents in Search of Information

Hoberman, Mary Ann. *Not Enough Beds for the Babies*. Illus. by Helen Spyer. Boston: Little, Brown & Co., 1965.
Ormondroyd, Edward. *Theodore*. Illus. by John Larrecq. Berkeley, Calif.: Parnassus Press, 1966.
Skorpen, Liesel. *Charles*. Illus. by the author. New York: Harper & Row, Publishers, Inc., 1971.
Supraner, Robyn. *Would You Rather Be a Tiger?* Illus. by Barbara Cooney. Boston: Houghton Mifflin, 1973.
Waber, Bernard. *Ira Sleeps Over*. Illus. by the author. Boston: Houghton Mifflin, 1972.
Wilson, Julia. *Becky*. Illus. by John Wilson. New York: Thomas Y. Crowell Co., 1966.
Zemach, Harve, and Margot Zemach. *Mommy, Buy Me a China Doll*. Illus. by Margot Zemach. Chicago: Follett Publishing Co., 1966.
Zolotow, Charlotte. *William's Doll*. Illus. by William Pene du Bois. New York: Harper & Row Publishers, Inc., 1972.

Fitting into Behavior Patterns

Behrens, June. *How I Feel*. Photographs by Vince Streano. Chicago: Childrens Press, 1973.
Conford, Ellen. *Why Can't I Be William?* Illus. by Philip Wande. Boston: Little, Brown & Co., 1972.
Dunn, Judy. *Feelings*. Photographs by Phoebe and Tris Dunn. Mankato, Minn.: Creative Educational Society, Inc., 1970.
Ets, Marie Hall. *Bad Boy, Good Boy*. Illus. by the author. New York: Thomas Y. Crowell Co., 1967.
Gackenbach, Dick. *Claude the Dog*. Illus. by the author. New York: Seabury Press, Inc., 1974.
Hoban, Russell. *The Little Brute Family*. Illus. by Lillian Hoban. New York: Macmillan Publishing Co., 1966.
———. *The Sorely Trying Day*. Illus. by Lillian Hoban. New York: Harper & Row Publishers, Inc., 1964.
Johnston, Johanna. *Speak Up, Edie!* Illus. by Paul Galdone. New York: G. P. Putnam's Sons, 1974.
Kessler, Leonard. *Did You Ever Hear a Klunk Say Please?* Illus. by the author. New York: Dodd, Mead & Co., 1967.
Kraus, Robert. *Rebecca Hatpin*. Illus. by Robert Byrd. New York: E. P. Dutton & Co., 1974.
Kuskin, Karla. *What Did You Bring Me?* Illus. by the author. New York: Harper & Row Publishers, Inc., 1973.
Potter, Beatrix. *The Tale of Peter Rabbit*. Illus. by the author. New York: Frederick Warne & Co., 1902.

Preston, Edna Mitchell. *The Temper Tantrum Book*. Illus. by Rainey Bennett. New York: Viking Press, 1969.

Sendak, Maurice. *Where the Wild Things Are*. Illus. by the author. New York: Harper & Row Publishers, Inc., 1963.

Shecter, Ben. *The Toughest and Meanest Kid on the Block*. Illus. by the author. New York: Harcourt Brace Jovanovich, Inc., 1973.

Sherman, Ivan. *I Do Not Like It When My Friend Comes to Visit*. Illus. by the author. New York: Harcourt Brace Jovanovich, Inc., 1973.

Simon, Norma. *I Was So Mad!* Illus. by Dora Leder. Chicago: Albert Whitman & Co., 1974.

Steptoe, John. *Stevie*. Illus. by the author. New York: Harper & Row Publishers, Inc., 1969.

Stover, Jo Ann. *If Everybody Did*. Illus. by the author. New York: David McKay Co., Inc., 1960.

Viorst, Judith. *Alexander and the Terrible, Horrible, No Good, Very Bad Day*. Illus. by Ray Cruz. New York: Atheneum Publishers, 1972.

Waber, Bernard. *Lyle and the Birthday Party*. Illus. by the author. Boston: Houghton Mifflin Co., 1966.

Watson, Jane. *Sometimes I'm Jealous*. Illus. by Hilde Hoffman. Racine, Wis.: Western Publishing Co., 1972.

Wells, Rosemary. *Benjamin & Tulip*. Illus. by the author. New York: Dial Press, 1973.

Zolotow, Charlotte. *The Hating Book*. Illus. by Ben Shecter. New York: Harper & Row Publishers, Inc., 1969.

———. *The Quarreling Book*. Illus. by Arnold Lobel. New York: Harper & Row Publishers, Inc., 1963.

Acquiring Self-Identity and Independence

Berger, Terry. *I Have Feelings*. Photographs by I. Howard Spivak. New York: Behavioral Press, 1971.

Cretan, Gladys. *Me, Myself and I*. Illus. by Don Bolognese. New York: William Morrow & Co., Inc., 1969.

De Regniers, Beatrice. *A Little House of Your Own*. Illus. by Irene Haas. New York: Harcourt Brace Jovanovich, Inc., 1955.

Gray, Genevieve. *Keep an Eye on Kevin: Safety Begins at Home*. Illus. by Don Madden. New York: Lothrop, Lee and Shepard Co., 1973.

Green, Mary. *Is It Hard? Is It Easy?* Photographs by Len Gittleman. Reading, Mass.: William R. Scott, Inc., 1960.

Heide, Florence. *Who Needs Me?* Illus. by Sally Mathews. Minneapolis: Augsburg Publishing House, 1971.

Hill, Elizabeth. *Evan's Corner*. Illus. by Nancy Grossman. New York: Holt, Rinehart & Winston, 1967.

Parents in Search of Information

Hoff, Syd. *My Aunt Rosie.* Illus. by the author. New York: Harper & Row Publishers, Inc., 1972.

Kessler, Leonard. *The Sad Tale of the Careless Klunks.* Illus. by the author. New York: Dodd, Mead & Co., 1965.

Klein, Norma. *Girls Can Be Anything.* Illus. by Roy Doty. New York: E. P. Dutton & Co., 1973.

Krasilovsky, Phyllis. *The Shy Little Girl.* Illus. by Trina Schart Hyman. Boston: Houghton Mifflin Co., 1970.

Kraus, Robert. *Leo the Late Bloomer.* Illus. by Jose Aruego. New York: Windmill Books, Inc., 1971.

Merriam, Eve. *Boys & Girls, Girls & Boys.* Illus. by Harriet Sherman. New York: Holt, Rinehart & Winston Co., 1972.

Poulet, Virginia. *Blue Bug's Safety Book.* Illus. by Donald Charles. Chicago: Childrens Press, 1973.

Shaw, Richard. *Who Are You Today?* Illus. by Kurt Werth. New York: Frederick Warne & Co., 1970.

Smaridge, Norah. *What a Silly Thing to Do.* Illus. by Susan Perl. Nashville: Abingdon Press, 1967.

Solot, Mary Lynn. *100 Hamburgers; the Getting Thin Book.* Illus. by Paul Galdone. New York: Lothrop, Lee & Shepard Co., 1972.

Sonneborn, Ruth. *The Lollipop Party.* Illus. by Brinton Turkle. New York: Viking Press, 1967.

Stanek, Muriel. *I Am Here.* Illus. by Jean Morey. Westchester, Ill.: Benefic Press, 1967.

———. *I Can Do It.* Illus. by Jean Morey. Westchester, Ill.: Benefic Press, 1967.

———. *Tall Tina.* Illus. by Lucy Hawkinson. Chicago: Albert Whitman & Co., 1970.

Stone, Elberta H. *I'm Glad I'm Me.* Illus. by Margery W. Brown. New York: G. P. Putnam's Sons, 1971.

Viorst, Judith. *Try It Again, Sam.* Illus. by Paul Galdone. New York: Lothrop, Lee & Shepard Co., 1970.

Yashima, Taro. *Umbrella.* Illus. by the author. New York: Viking Press, 1958.

Zolotow, Charlotte. *Someday.* Illus. by Arnold Lobel. New York: Harper & Row Publishers, Inc., 1965.

Developing Interests and Imagination

Fox, Paula. *Maurice's Room.* Illus. by the author. New York: Macmillan Publishing Co., 1966.

Kirtland, Susanne. *Easy Answers to Hard Questions.* Illus. by Susan Perl. New York: Grosset & Dunlap, 1969.

Kraus, Robert. *Leo the Late Bloomer.* Illus. by Jose Aruego. New York: Windmill Books, Inc., 1971.

Parenting Collection

by Grace W. Ruth

Small collections of books and pamphlets related to all aspects of early childhood can be a valuable and effective addition to children's library collections. Adult materials dealing with young children and early childhood education were first purchased as part of the Early Childhood Project collection of the San Francisco Public Library. One of the goals of this new Parenting Collection was to gather in one location materials from many different areas of the adult collection, as well as materials not previously represented in the library.

Patron response to the collection was positive, and children's librarians in the branches began to express the need for having similar, but smaller, collections of adult materials available for the increasing numbers of parents, students, and other adults who work with preschool children. Parents, especially, were requesting more books about parenting and the relationship of the young child to his total environment. As a result, small Parenting Collections were established in the children's rooms of all branches. The collection is designated reference material, so that titles are on hand at all times. Circulating copies of the books may be obtained from the adult collections.

The titles selected answer the most frequently asked questions concerning young children. There are books containing information about all areas of

Grace W. Ruth is Children's Specialist, Early Education Project, San Francisco Public Library.

growth and development and books dealing with various programs that involve young children—educational, adoptive, and so forth. For example:

General child rearing: Gruenberg, Sidonie Matsner, ed. *New Encyclopedia of Child Care and Guidance.* New York: Doubleday & Co., Inc., 1968.

Emotional development: Salk, Lee, and Kramer, Rita. *How to Raise a Human Being.* New York: Random House, 1969.

Social development: Goodman, Mary Ellen. *Race Awareness in Young Children.* rev. ed. New York: Macmillan Publishing Co., 1964.

Intellectual development: Chess, Stella. *Your Child Is a Person.* New York: Viking Press, 1972.

Discipline: Ginott, Haim. *Between Parent and Child.* New York: Macmillan Publishing Co., 1965.

Physical development: Prudden, Suzy. *Creative Fitness for Baby and Child.* New York: William Morrow & Co., 1972.

Play: Stein, Susan M., and Lottick, Sarah T. *Three, Four, Open the Door: Creative Fun for Young Children.* Chicago: Follett Publishing Co., 1971.

Special development: Spock, Benjamin, and Lerrigo, Marion. *Caring for Your Disabled Child.* New York: Macmillan Publishing Co., 1965.

Early childhood education:

Bruner, Jerome S. *The Relevance of Education.* New York: W. W. Norton & Co., Inc., 1971.

Curtis, Jean. *Parents' Guide to Nursery Schools.* New York: Random House, 1971.

Orem, R. C. *Montessori Today.* New York: G. P. Putnam's Sons, 1971.

Children's rights: Holt, John. *Escape from Childhood.* New York: E. P. Dutton & Co., Inc., 1974.

Pamphlets were selected to supplement the book collection. Many are quite inexpensive and can be readily purchased by adults for home reference. Some pamphlets provide a good, brief summary of their subject:

Children's Bureau, U.S. Dept. of Health, Education, and Welfare. *Your Child from 1 to 6.* Washington, D.C.: Govt. Printing Office, 1962.

Hymes, James L., Jr. *Early Childhood Education: An Introduction to the Profession.* Washington, D.C.: National Association for the Education of Young Children, 1968.

This pamphlet deals with the many types of preschool programs in operation: Head Start, day care centers, nursery schools, etc.

Some pamphlets provide information not available in books, or the most current information on a subject:

Bureau of Product Safety, U.S. Dept. of Health, Education, and Welfare. *Toy Safety.* Washington, D.C.: Govt. Printing Office, 1972.

Felker, Evelyn H. *Foster Parenting Young Children: Guidelines from a Foster Parent.* New York: Child Welfare League of America, Inc., 1974.

Found Spaces and Equipment for Children's Centers. New York: Educational Facilities Laboratories, Inc., 1972.

MacEwan, Phyllis Taube. *Liberating Young Children from Sex Roles.* Boston: The New England Free Press, 1972.

Office of Child Development. *Caring for Children* series, vols. 1– (10 publ. to date; series no. HE21-210:1–10). Washington, D.C.: Govt. Printing Office, 1970– .

Rohr, Franz. *How Parents Tell Children They Are Adopted.* Sacramento, Calif.: Children's Home Society of California, 1970.

Reference order lists of thirty-two books and eighteen pamphlets were prepared by the staff of the Early Childhood Project. Branch librarians ordered those titles that would be most useful in their individual neighborhoods. At the same time, the titles were available on an adult subject order list, to become part of the adult circulating collections. Thus, adults expressing interest in a particular title can be referred by the children's librarian to the circulating copy in the adult collection. Additional paperback copies might also be purchased for circulation from children's rooms. Librarians may also want to keep a list of the titles available in paperback and information on where they can be purchased.

Children's librarians set up a special shelf or section for the Parenting Collection and called attention to it by display, sign, or individual introduction. An especially good place to shelve the collection is above the picture stories, at parents' eye level. The collection is also introduced at talks to parent groups. The adult response was immediate and positive, but continued introduction by the children's librarian is needed for continued use of the materials.

The Parenting Collection is most heavily used by parents of preschoolers, as well as by day care and nursery school personnel and students in high school and college level child care and parenting classes. Among the most popular titles are:

Fraiberg, Selma. *The Magic Years.* New York: Charles Scribner's Sons, 1968.

Gordon, Thomas. *P.E.T. Parent Effectiveness Training.* New York: Wyden, Inc., 1970.

Marzollo, Jean, and Janice Lloyd. *Learning through Play.* New York: Harper and Row Publishers, Inc., 1972.

There is also an increasing need to include materials on ethnic groups and

Parents in Search of Information

in languages other than English, particularly on the subject of child rearing. Some pamphlet materials are available in Spanish, and books include such titles as:

Harrison-Ross, Phyllis, and Barbara Wyden. *The Black Child: A Parent's Guide.* New York: Wyden, Inc., 1973.

Kao, Ching Lang. *The Chinese Skillful Doctors' Analysis: A New Treatment of Childhood Illness.* Hong Kong: Van-Yep Publishing Company, n.d.

Spock, Benjamin. *Tu Hijo.* 6th ed. (Spanish translation of *Baby and Child Care.*) Madrid: Daimon, 1963.

A Public Library Program Series for Parents of Preschool Children

by Mary Anne Corrier

A common problem at the first of a series of preschool story hours is separating parents and children. Each group, it seems, experiences some hesitancy at abandoning the other. And understandably so. For both groups it is usually the first experience with the children's library. The individual three-year-old may be confused by the other children—all strangers, the new routine required by the storyteller, or the general newness of the situation. The parent may not have prepared the child for the separation.

The adults, also, may feel a little uncertain. They may have been borrowing library materials for their children, but now they question the expertise of the librarian in charge of a program for such young children. Maybe they've heard about the program from friends and decided to give it a try.

Whatever the reasons for the patrons' presence or their hesitancy, the librarian is presented with two curious and receptive audiences—the children and their parents. For perhaps thirty to forty-five minutes both groups will be in the library. Most children's librarians have no problem in devising activities for six or eight sessions with preschoolers, but the prospect of an equal amount of time spent with the children's parents may seem overpowering. A joint series could provide an opportunity to introduce parent and child to a variety of library materials, by providing selected examples and by demonstrating the recreational and educational value of library media.

To administer a dual program, several elements are necessary: potential parent interest, willing staff, adequate hardware and software or the ability to improvise, a knowledge of the community, and careful consideration of the

Mary Anne Corrier is a children's librarian in the Bloomingdale Branch, The New York Public Library, New York City.

services and information a preschool parent may find helpful. Mothers of pre-school youngsters are certainly interested in materials for their children, but they may be equally enthusiastic about sessions that deal solely with adult materials. Sometimes a librarian may find that a film or book talk related to the adults' interests provides the parents with a pleasant change from their child-centered world.

Staff

Are there several people who usually work in the children's room or will other staff members need to be recruited? Is there an adult staff member who would consider the parents' program as part of his or her domain? Is someone on the staff able to operate a film projector? Is there someone on the staff who enjoys crafts or music and would be willing to help with one or two sessions? If some of the parents are non-English speaking, are there enough staff who are bilingual to participate in a joint program?

For each session three people will be needed. One person will conduct the children's group, one will conduct the adult session, and one should be available to deal with whatever problems arise. For example, a child who has no one to take him to the bathroom can disrupt the most professionally planned program.

Community

Community needs should also be considered in scheduling the programs for parents. Would weekday mornings be more convenient for the adults? Preschoolers are usually freshest in the morning, and older children are in school at that time. In communities where parents may have to drive several miles to the library, Saturday might be a wise choice. Perhaps the working parent would then have the opportunity to attend. Some libraries may find the best time for the adult program is in the evening, independent of the children's program. If staff is limited, parents might come on alternate nights, and library personnel would not be committed to handling a child and an adult program simultaneously.

What community resources can be tapped? Is there a health agency that can provide a lecturer on nutrition or child care? Is there a local author, an illustrator, artist, or craftsperson who might contribute time for one session? Is there someone from the police department who would be willing to discuss a topic such as neighborhood crime prevention? Community resource people may be scheduled to meet the needs of a particular group of parents or they may be used for enrichment.

Careful consideration should be given to the particular library's relationship to the community before the program is initiated. If the staff feels that it is not sure of the needs and resources in its community, perhaps time could be spent profitably in identifying these concerns before planning a series of parent programs. The pamphlet *Libraries: Centers for Children's Needs* would be a useful tool in beginning this evaluation.

Equipment and Materials

As plans are developed for a series of parent programs, careful consideration should be given to the availability of equipment and materials. If the library planning parent programs does not own films, is there a resource center from which they may be borrowed? If films are included in a program series, provision must also be made for a screen and a projector of the correct millimeter. If a simultaneous program is planned in which records or cassettes are to be used, are there at least two record or cassette players available? Is there enough time to gather materials for crafts demonstrations? Access to mimeograph machines is desirable, so bibliographies can be distributed at the close of each session. Are there funds to buy needed materials? If money is extremely limited, a staff may decide to use print materials solely.

Program

Consideration of the interests of the parents, community resources, library resources, and staff size and expertise should help determine the form a program will take. If the parents' sessions are to be held simultaneously with the preschool program, it would seem wise to relate the adults' material to that used in the children's group. Parent and child then have the opportunity to reinforce each other's experiences. Furthermore, the task of selecting program topics that would interest a possibly diverse group would be eliminated.

Here are some suggested thirty-five-minute sessions for a typical eight-week series. These ideas are not meant to be definitive but only to serve as a guide to developing programs suited to individual communities. A bibliography is provided at the end of the article.

FIRST ADULT SESSION

If the children are very young, parents could be permitted to attend the first preschool session. It should be made clear to both groups that this arrangement is for the first session only.

Some librarians may prefer to begin the program series by helping parents realize the value of reading with their children. An assistant might show the film *The Pleasure Is Mutual.* A film program frees staff to concentrate on the children for the first session, often a hectic one.

If staffing permits, the children's librarian or other qualified person might discuss what makes a good picture book for preschoolers. This presentation could include the reading of a few titles suitable for three-year-olds, and several aimed at four- and five-year-olds, demonstrating the differences between the two groups.

Parents in Search of Information

Bibliographies should be distributed at the conclusion of the first program. The bibliography should feature the books mentioned in the film or those read, as well as provide titles for background reading. The books listed should be readily available for the parents to browse through. During the browsing period a staff member might check to see that all the adults have library cards.

SECOND SESSION
Arrange for the children to listen to selections from recordings and/or sing in addition to listening to the stories which will be read. In the parent program, plan a discussion of rhyming and word use by young children. Chukovsky's *From Two to Five* should be helpful in planning the session. Ask the parents if the children have any favorite rhymes or words that they enjoy experimenting with. Mention the significance of these words as indicators of a child's language development.

The librarian might then point out the use of rhythm and rhyme as mnemonic devices and introduce materials that help children develop their ability to memorize, such as simple singing games, nursery rhymes, and nonsense verse. This would be the time to play a few selections from recordings by such artists as Burl Ives or Ella Jenkins. The Sesame Street records and song book would also fit nicely here. If preferred, some picture song books such as *Fox Went Out on a Chilly Night* or *John Henry* may be used in this part of the discussion.

The session might be concluded by a discussion among parents and staff of the songs both groups have found successful with young children. Mention the relationship of singing, rhythm, and rhyme to poetry, as a preview of the coming week's session. A bibliography should be distributed.

THIRD SESSION
Plan for the children to use rhythm instruments in addition to their other activities. For the parents, the use of poetry with children would make a logical program to follow last week's session. Introduce various editions of Mother Goose but add such titles as *Some of the Days of Everett Anderson, Father Fox's Pennyrhymes,* or *In a Spring Garden.* It should be stressed that to be really appreciated poems have to be heard. The young child's ear is attuned to rhyme, and the preschool years are the time to initiate a love of poems read aloud. Other picture books, written in verse, might also be introduced. If the group seems relaxed, discussion and participation could be encouraged.

An alternate adult program might be one devoted to making and using rhythm instruments with children. John Hawkinson's *Music and Instruments for Children to Make* would be useful, along with selections from recordings, to give a concrete idea of ways to use rhythm instruments. A staff member can give a brief explanation of each instrument and then allow the adults to work while the remainder of the lecture continues.

A Public Library Program Series

Once again bibliographies should be distributed and books made available at the conclusion of the session.

FOURTH SESSION

This might be the day to introduce a guest speaker. The person selected may be a community service speaker, a local craftsperson, or an author.

If a speaker is not scheduled, plan a program on simple crafts. Projects demonstrated must be interesting enough for the children to enjoy, but uncomplicated and clean enough to be feasible for a parent with a preschooler and perhaps an infant at home. The series by James Razzi or Betsy Pflug's *Funny Bags* provide some workable projects. Materials should be available for staff to demonstrate examples.

In communities where a museum is located, someone from that staff might be contacted and asked to provide an introduction to their adult education and children's programs.

FIFTH SESSION

Free! Parents may be thankful to browse for a half hour in the adult or children's department without the responsibility of their children. Coffee might be served to encourage parents to remain in the library to discuss the program with the staff and other parents. Books and materials used in previous sessions, as well as related items, should be attractively displayed.

SIXTH SESSION

Try a film. This might be something purely entertaining or it might be a film of community interest. Some librarians may choose to alternate preschool related sessions with those geared to adult topics. Others may find that attendance often diminishes toward the end of the series and may wish to schedule the preschool topics first.

SEVENTH SESSION

One of the staff from the adult department might do short book talks. Or the program might be shared by a guest speaker and a librarian who will select books on the speaker's topic.

EIGHTH SESSION

This is the last session of the series. If possible, serve coffee or other light refreshments to encourage the parents to linger and, perhaps, help the staff with an evaluation of the program. Some library systems may require a formal evaluation of such a program. Whatever the case, use this last session to answer any questions the group might have and to solicit their opinions on the content of the series.

Parents in Search of Information

The children will be attending their last session today also. When they join their parents some small happy occasion should be created. They might be given their name tags to take home and some juice or milk as a surprise.

Obviously, a parents' series such as this one takes planning and thought. As a first requirement, the children's program should be well organized. Perhaps two series could be held before the simultaneous programming is initiated. Publicity should stress that the purpose of the joint series is to introduce the preschooler and his parents to library materials by providing selected examples. The recreational aspect of this dual adventure shouldn't be ignored either.

After an eight-week dual program it's not unusual for preschool parents to be counted among a library's most loyal supporters. There's something about seeing a young child bound into a library and run for the picture books that gives both staff and parents a common bond of accomplishment. Most parents no longer feel overwhelmed by the multitude of materials available to their children. Over a period of eight weeks, relationships among staff, parents, and children are formed and usually continue as long as the family stays in the neighborhood. For this dividend alone, the program is worth the planning and extra thought.

The following suggested titles are meant only as guides. Recordings, cassettes, and 16mm. films are included for those who may wish to use them. The Spanish-language material recommended here has been selected for use where the parent programs would be most effective conducted in that language.

Bibliography

FILMS

The Lively Art of Picture Books. Color. 57 min. 16mm. Weston, Conn.: Weston Woods, 1964.

An examination of picture books, their meaning to children and to the authors and illustrators who create them. Includes visits to the studios of Robert McCloskey, Maurice Sendak, and Barbara Cooney.

The Pleasure Is Mutual. Color. 24 min. 16mm. Westport, Conn.: Connecticut Films, 1966.

Provides an opportunity for parents who have never seen a picture book program the opportunity to see parts of ten different programs. The children's enjoyment of the programs is most evident and the different styles of the storytellers should be most reassuring.

BACKGROUND BOOKS

Chukovsky, Korei. *From Two to Five.* Translated by Miriam Morton. Berkeley: University of California Press, 1963.

The Russian children's poet provides insight into the language development, thought processes, and imagination of the very young child.

Lanes, Selma G. *Down the Rabbit Hole*. New York: Atheneum Publishers, 1971.

Critical essays on various aspects of children's literature. Several of these should be of interest to parents beginning their journey through preschool picture books.

Smith, Lillian H. *The Unreluctant Years*. Chicago: American Library Association, 1953.

Areas of children's literature are covered individually as the author proposes critical standards for judging each type. The section on picture books would be very useful to the parents of a preschooler.

Taylor, Barbara J. *A Child Goes Forth*. Provo, Utah: Brigham Young University Press, 1964.

Subtitled "A curriculum guide for teachers of preschool children," the text provides an almost inexhaustible source of activities for the preschool child. Most of these could be adapted to the library or home. For the parent who wishes to pursue the subject further, bibliographies are included at the end of each chapter.

BOOKS FOR THREE-YEAR-OLDS

Hoban, Tana. *Count and See*. New York: Macmillan Publishing Co., 1972.

Hutchins, Pat. *Rosie's Walk*. New York: Macmillan Publishing Co., 1968.

Kraus, Robert. *Whose Mouse Are You?* New York: Macmillan Publishing Co., 1968.

Munari, Bruno. *ABC*. New York: World Publishing Co., 1960.

——. *The Elephant's Wish*. New York: World Publishing Co., 1959.

——. *Who's There? Open the Door*. New York: World Publishing Co., 1957.

Nakano, Hirotaka. *Elephant Blue*. Indianapolis: Bobbs-Merrill Company, 1970.

Sendak, Maurice. *Pierre*. New York: Harper and Row Publishers, Inc., 1962.

BOOKS FOR FOUR-YEAR-OLDS

Brown, Marcia. *The Three Billy Goats Gruff*. New York: Harcourt Brace Jovanovich, 1972.

Freeman, Don. *Corduroy*. New York: Viking Press, 1968.

Keats, Ezra Jack. *Whistle for Willie*. New York: Viking Press, 1964.

Kraus, Robert. *Milton the Early Riser*. New York: Windmill Books, 1972.

Massie, Diane R. *The Baby Beebee Bird*. New York: Harper and Row Publishers, Inc., 1963.

Sendak, Maurice. *Where the Wild Things Are*. New York: Harper and Row Publishers, Inc., 1963.

Slobodkina, Esphyr. *Caps for Sale*. New York: Young Scott, 1947.

Parents in Search of Information

Suteyev, V. *Three Kittens.* New York: Crown Publishers, 1973.
Viorst, Judith. *Alexander and the Terrible, Horrible, No Good, Very Bad Day.* New York: Atheneum Publishers, 1972.
Vipont, Elfrida. *The Elephant and the Bad Baby.* New York: Coward, McCann & Geoghegan, 1970.
Withers, Carl. *The Tale of the Black Cat.* New York: Holt, Rinehart & Winston, 1973.
Zacharias, Thomas. *But Where Is the Green Parrot?* New York: Delacorte Press, 1968.

MUSIC WITH PARENTS

Hawkinson, John, and Martha Faulhaber. *Music and Instruments for Children to Make.* Chicago: Albert Whitman & Co., 1970.
John Henry: An American Legend. Illustrated by Ezra Jack Keats. New York: Pantheon Books, 1965.
Landeck, Beatrice. *More Songs to Grow On.* New York: William Morrow & Co., 1954.
————, and Elizabeth Crook. *Wake Up and Sing.* New York: William Morrow & Co., 1969.
Langstaff, John, and Feodor Rojankovsky. *Frog Went a-Courtin'.* New York: Harcourt Brace Jovanovich, 1955.
Langstaff, John. *Over in the Meadow.* New York: Harcourt Brace Jovanovich, 1957.
Mandell, Muriel, and Robert E. Wood. *Make Your Own Musical Instruments.* New York: Sterling, 1957.
Mitchell, Donald. *Every Child's Book of Nursery Songs.* New York: Crown Publishers, 1969.
Moss, Jeffrey, and Joseph G. Raposo. *The Sesame Street Song Book.* New York: Simon & Schuster, 1971.
Thomas, Marlo. *Free to Be... You and Me.* New York: McGraw-Hill Book Co., 1974.

POETRY WITH PARENTS

Clifton, Lucille. *Some of the Days of Everett Anderson.* New York: Holt, Rinehart & Winston, 1970.
DeRegniers, Beatrice Schenk. *May I Bring a Friend?* New York: Atheneum Publishers, 1964.
Ivimey, John William. *Complete Version of Ye Three Blind Mice.* New York: Frederick Warne & Co., 1909.
Mother Goose
  The Tall Book of Mother Goose. Illus. by Feodor Rojankovsky. New York: Harper & Row Publishers, Inc., 1942.

A Public Library Program Series

The Mother Goose Treasury. Illus. by Raymond Briggs. New York: Coward-McCann & Geoghegan, 1966.
Mother Goose, Seventy-seven Verses. Illus. by Tasha Tudor. New York: Henry Z. Walck, 1944.
Sendak, Maurice. *Pierre.* New York: Harper and Row Publishers, Inc., 1962.
Watson, Clyde. *Father Fox's Pennyrhymes.* New York: Thomas Y. Crowell Co., 1971.

ARTS AND CRAFTS WITH PARENTS

Bland, Jane Cooper. *Art of the Young Child: Understanding and Encouraging Creative Growth in Children Three to Five.* New York: Museum of Modern Art, 1968.
Pflug, Betsy. *Funny Bags.* New York: Van Nostrand, 1968.
Razzi, James. *Bag of Tricks.* New York: Parents' Magazine Press, 1971.
———. *Easy Does It.* New York: Parents' Magazine Press, 1969.
———. *Simply Fun.* New York: Parents' Magazine Press, 1968.
Seidelman, James E. *Shopping Cart Art.* New York: Macmillan Book Co., 1970.

USEFUL PAMPHLETS

Office for Library Service to the Disadvantaged. *Libraries: Centers for Children's Needs.* Chicago: American Library Association, 1974.
   A practical guide to gathering community resource information for library use and reader referral.
Conwell, Mary K. and Pura Belpré. *Libros en Español.* New York: New York Public Library. Office of Children's Services, 1971.
   Bibliography of United States and foreign children's books in Spanish. Features bilingual annotations; a list of vendors is included.
Foster, Joanne. *How to Conduct Effective Picture Book Programs: A Handbook.* White Plains, N.Y.: Westchester Library System, 1967 ($2.50 prepaid).
   Intended for use in training storytellers in the art of presenting picture book programs, this booklet contains valuable information for anyone interested in young children and their literature. Anne Izard served as consultant for this handbook and for the film *The Pleasure Is Mutual* (Connecticut Films). The pamphlet and film are intended to be used together, although each may be used independently.

RECORDS AND CASSETTES

Burl Ives Sings Little White Duck and Other Children's Favorites. Harmony: HS 14507.
Glazer, Tom (comp.) *Activity and Game Songs.* CMS Records: CMS657, 658.

Parents in Search of Information

Guthrie, Woody. *Songs to Grow On.* Folkways Records: FC7501.
Jenkins, Ella. *You'll Sing a Song and I'll Sing a Song.* Folkways Records: FC7501. (Cassette: Folkways/Scholastic FC 60105.)
Peter, Paul and Mommy. Warner Brothers-Seven Arts Records: WS1785. (Cassette: Warner Brothers/Seven Arts CWX 1785.)
Marching Along Together. Decca: DL 74450.
Schwartz, Tony. *1, 2, 3, and a Zing, Zing, Zing.* Folkways Records: FC7003.
Sesame Street. RCA Camden: CAS 1127. (Cassette: Columbia 16 10 1069.)
Sesame Street 2. Warner Brothers Records: BS 2569
Thomas, Marlo. *Free to Be... You and Me.* Bell Records: Bell 1110.

MATERIALS IN SPANISH

Picture Books

Belpré, Pura. *Oté.* New York: Pantheon Books, 1969.
> An old Puerto Rican folktale about a poor peasant and his encounter with the devil.

Belpré, Pura. *Pérez y Martina.* New York: Frederick Warne & Co., 1966.
> The story of Martina, a Spanish cockroach, and Pérez, "a gallant little mouse."

Frasconi, Antonio. *The Snow and the Sun. La Nieve y el Sol.* New York: Harcourt Brace Jovanovich, 1961.
> A South American folk rhyme in Spanish and English.

Gargante, José and María Luisa Jover. *Yo Soy el Rojo. Yo Soy el Amarillo. Yo Soy el Azul.* Barcelona: LaGalera, 1968.
> An attractive series on colors for the preschooler.

Jiménez-Landi, Antonio. *ABC... XYZ.* Madrid: Aguilar, 1967.
> An alphabet book that follows the adventure of a little burro.

Leaf, Munro. *El Cuento de Ferdinando.* New York: Viking Press, 1962.
> A translation of the story of the young bull who prefers flowers to fighting.

Lenski, Lois. *El Auto Pequeño. La Granja Pequeña. Papá Pequeño. Vaquero Pequeño.* New York: Henry Z. Walck, 1968.
> Translations of the Lenski favorites.

Lionni, Leo. *Suimi.* New York: Pantheon Books, 1963.
> *Swimmy* translated into Spanish.

Minarik, Else. *Osito.* New York: Harper & Row Publishers, Inc., 1969.
> The adventures of *Little Bear* in Spanish.

Poesías de la Madre Oca. New York: Thomas Y. Crowell Co., 1968.
> Mother Goose rhymes in Spanish, with appropriate illustrations by Barbara Cooney.

Rey, Hans A. *Jorge el Curioso.* Boston: Houghton Mifflin, 1961.
> A translation of *Curious George.*

Songs

Prieto, Mariana Beeching de (comp.) *Play It in Spanish.* New York: John Day Co., 1973.

Seventeen games and action songs from Latin America, Spain, and the West Indies.

Yurchenco, Henrietta. *A Fiesta of Folk Songs from Spain and Latin America.* New York: G. P. Putnam's Sons, 1967.

Songs from Spain and Latin America, with words and music.

Records

Glazer, Tom. *Children's Songs from Latin America.* CMS Records: CMS 659.

Yurchenco, Henrietta (comp.) *Songs and Games from Mexico and Puerto Rico.* Asch Recordings: AHS 751.

Crafts

Sainz-Pardo, Manuel. *Juega y Construye.* Hightstown, N.J.: Santillana Publishing Co., 1963.

A practical book on how to make things with materials found around the home.

*Visits to the library encourage child-adult interaction.
Photo, taken at Evansville (Ind.) Public Library,
courtesy Evansville (Ind.) Press.*

PART 5

Opening More Doors

Puzzle the child a bit, bewilder him a bit,
set him guessing, groping,
force him to think and feel a little above himself.

Clifton Fadiman
"Party of One"
Holiday, August, 1952, p. 9

The School Library and the Kindergarten

by Nancy B. Christensen

I know a place ... ," said Andrew to Tim in Crosby Bonsall's *Tell Me Some More* (Harper & Row), "where I can hold an elephant under my arm.... In this place ... I can be taller than a tree, bigger than a ship, wider than a whale.... In this place ... I can pick up a river and never get wet at all." Some fortunate kindergarten children know this special place—the school library; and they also know the person who can satisfy their curiosity and help to make books and reading an exciting adventure. And kindergarten teachers, too, know that the school library can provide their children with many supportive and enriching services.

For the teacher, the librarian is the source of materials for all aspects of the instructional program. The librarian, familiar with the kindergarten curriculum, selects suitable materials for purchase and suggests to the teacher those which are appropriate for specific needs. For example, a duck-hatching project, beginning with duck embryology and terminating with the bird's migration, requires a wealth of resources. Geraldine Flanagan's *Window into an Egg* (Young Scott) and books like *How Life Begins* by Jules Power (Simon & Schuster) are important; but a host of other materials—story books, films, pictures, filmstrips, science books, and recordings—should be used. Children can ask countless questions when the activity is concerned with growth and development. They want to know if their own blood is like that of the duck; they are curious about the duck's father and mother, what ducks eat, where they go in winter, and why one has died before it is fully hatched. The bibliography for a single project can be extensive.

Nancy Christensen is a kindergarten teacher at the Maria Hastings School, Lexington, Massachusetts.

Opening More Doors

It is important for the kindergarten teacher and the school librarian to co-operate in organizing a program, because the library offers many learning opportunities for young children. It serves as an extension of the classroom in many ways. Ideally, class time should be scheduled in the library when the librarian is free to devote her full attention to the children. By offering a regular time for the boys and girls to browse and listen to a story, the librarian gives them all a chance to see a wide variety of books and listen to an experienced storyteller. Although a daily story time is a part of the kindergarten schedule, most children are delighted with a tale told in a library setting. They delight in retelling the story later as they show others the pictures in the book. Anyone who knows *Mike's House* by Julia Sauer (Viking) is aware of how possessively a young child will cling to a favorite story.

In addition to regular visits by the whole class, small groups and individual children should be encouraged to use the library to seek information on subjects of personal interest. Every day a child, clutching in his hand a butterfly, a caterpillar, a seashell, or a stone, will make his way to the library to find answers to his questions about a newly acquired treasure. What satisfaction when the librarian can provide simple information, and perhaps a picture, of a precious possession!

The teacher and the librarian should plan additional programs according to the needs of the children. For instance, the kindergarten boy or girl who knows how to read should have an individually designed library program to enhance his interest in books. It is important for the teacher to be aware of the child's comprehension level and provide an opportunity for him to retell a story in sequence; and it is wise for the teacher and the librarian to discuss both the child and his books in order to meet his interests and his developing needs.

As soon as the children are acquainted with the librarian and the routines of the library, they should begin to borrow books. Sue Felt's *Rosa-Too-Little* (Doubleday) is an excellent story to read to a kindergarten class before they begin to borrow library books. Kindergartners feel proud and important when they carry books home, as their older sister and brother do. To prepare for borrowing materials, the librarian can provide the class with blank cards, so the children can practice printing their names or at least their initials. This simple procedure teaches children a great deal about sharing and about assuming responsibility. When a child brings his book home, the family can be involved in his education. Some children like to return a book as soon as it has been read; others prefer to keep it for a week so it can be read over and over again.

In addition to being consumers of books, children can be encouraged to make their own books by acting as authors and illustrators. A homemade book—dictated by the children and written down by the teacher—may be only a few pages long with a large picture and one or two sentences on each page, but it should be duplicated and made available to other children in the library. Not only have the kindergartners created and verbalized a story, but they have also gained their first insights into the production of books.

Children gain respect for sources of information by their contacts with the library and the librarian. The library fosters an appreciation of books and an enjoyment of reading. Programs especially designed for the kindergarten contribute to the child's integration into the total life of the school and assure continuity in succeeding years, since the same librarian will usually guide the child through his entire elementary school experience. Thus, the librarian has a unique opportunity to build a foundation for continuing library use and to help young children become lifetime learners.

Library Books for the Kindergarten

Birnbaum, Abe. *Green Eyes.* Racine, Wis.: Western Publishing Company, 1973.

Bishop, Claire. *Five Chinese Brothers.* New York: Coward, McCann & Geoghegan, 1938.

Brown, Margaret Wise. *Dead Bird.* Reading, Mass.: Addison-Wesley, 1958.

Burton, Virginia Lee. *Mike Mulligan and His Steam Shovel.* Boston: Houghton Mifflin, 1939.

Careme, Maurice. *Mother Raspberry.* Illus. by Marie Wabbles. New York: Thomas Y. Crowell Co., 1969.

Credle, Ellis. *Down, Down the Mountain.* Illus. by the author. Nashville, Tenn.: Thomas Nelson, Inc., 1971.

Duvoisin, Roger. *House of Four Seasons.* New York: Lothrop, Lee & Shepard Co., 1956.

———. *Veronica.* Illus. by the author. New York: Alfred A. Knopf, Inc., 1961

Flack, Marjorie. *Ask Mr. Bear.* New York: Macmillan Publishing Co., 1958.

Freeman, Don. *Corduroy.* New York: Viking Press, 1968.

Gauch, Patricia Lee. *Christina Katerina and the Box.* New York: Coward, McCann & Geoghegan, 1971.

———. *Christina Katerina and the First Annual Grand Ballet.* new ed. Illus. by Doris Burn. New York: Coward, McCann & Geoghegan, 1973.

Graham, Margaret B. *Be Nice to Spiders.* New York: Harper & Row, Publishers, Inc., 1967.

Gretz, Susanna. *Teddy Bears, One to Ten.* Illus. by the author. Chicago: Follett Publishing Co., 1970.

Hoban, Russell. *Bedtime for Frances.* Illus. by Garth Williams. New York: Harper & Row, Publishers, Inc., 1960.

Hutchins, Pat. *Changes, Changes.* Illus. by the author. New York: Macmillan Publishing Co., 1971.

Opening More Doors

Janosch. *Just One Apple.* New York: Henry Z. Walck, 1966.

Keats, Ezra Jack. *Snowy Day.* New York: Viking Press, 1962.

———. *Whistle for Willie.* New York: Viking Press, 1964.

Kempner, Carol. *Nicholas.* New York: Simon & Schuster, 1968.

Krasilovsky, Phyllis. *Very Little Boy.* Illus. by Ninon. Garden City, N.Y.: Doubleday & Co., Inc., 1962.

———. *Very Little Girl.* Illus. by Ninon. Garden City, N.Y.: Doubleday & Co., Inc., 1953.

Krauss, Ruth. *Growing Story.* Illus. by Phyllis Rowand. New York: Harper & Row, Publishers, Inc., 1947.

Lionni, Leo. *Little Blue and Little Yellow.* Illus. by the author. Stamford, Conn.: Astor-Honor, 1959.

———. *Swimmy.* Illus. by the author. New York: Pantheon Books, 1963.

Lipkind, William and Mordvinoff, Nicolas. *Finders Keepers.* Illus. by Nicolas Mordvinoff. New York: Harcourt Brace Jovanovich, 1951.

Livermore, Elaine. *Find the Cat.* Illus. by the author. Boston: Houghton Mifflin Co., 1973.

———. *One to Ten, Count Again.* Boston: Houghton Mifflin Co., 1973.

Mosel, Arlene. *Tikki, Tikki, Tembo.* Illus. by Blair Lent. New York: Holt, Rinehart & Winston, 1968.

Olschewski, Alfred. *Wheel Rolls Over.* Boston: Little, Brown & Co., 1962.

Potter, Beatrix. *Peter Rabbit.* New York: Frederick Warne & Co., 1902.

———. *Tale of Benjamin Bunny.* New York: Frederick Warne & Co., 1904.

Rey, Margaret and Rey, H. A. *Curious George Goes to the Hospital.* Boston: Houghton Mifflin Co., 1966.

Rockwell, Anne. *Toolbox.* Illus. by Harlow Rockwell. New York: Macmillan Publishing Co., 1971.

Showers, Paul. *Look at Your Eyes.* Illus. by Paul Galdone. New York: Thomas Y. Crowell Co., 1962.

———. *Your Skin and Mine.* Illus. by Paul Galdone. New York: Thomas Y. Crowell Co., 1965.

Udry, Janice M. *What Mary Jo Shared.* Illus. by Eleanor Mill. Chicago: Albert Whitman & Co., 1966.

Ungerer, Tomi. *Snail, Where Are You?* Illus. by the author. New York: Harper & Row, Publishers, Inc., 1962.

Ward, Lynd. *Biggest Bear.* Boston: Houghton Mifflin Co., 1952.

Welber, Robert. *Winter Picnic.* Illus. by Deborah Ray. New York: Pantheon Books, 1970.

Young, Miriam. *If I Drove a Car.* Illus. by Robert Quackenbush. New York: Lothrop, Lee & Shepard Co., 1971.

Zion, Gene. *Harry the Dirty Dog.* Illus. by Margaret B. Graham. New York: Harper & Row, Publishers, Inc., 1956.

————. *No Roses for Harry.* Illus. by Margaret B. Graham. New York: Harper & Row, Publishers, Inc., 1958.

References

Cianciolo, Patricia Jean. "Use Wordless Picture Books to Teach Reading, Visual Literacy, and to Study Literature," *Top of the News* 29:226–34 (April 1973).

Fitzgerald, Irene. "Literature Approved by Today's Kindergarten Children," *Elementary English* 68:953–59 (December 1971).

Parker, Patricia. "What Comes after Mother Goose?" *Elementary English* 64:505–10 (April 1969).

Wilkins, Lea-Ruth C. "Kindergarten Children in the Library—It's Theirs, Too!" *School Library Journal* 21:28–30 (April 1975).

The Library Door Is Open

by Ferne Johnson and Jacqueline Morris

Preschool and parent services are vital library functions. "The close relationship between reading and all of a child's language and life experiences means that everyone who works with the child, whether in or out of school, can affect learning."[1] In the last ten years, educators—including children's librarians—have become increasingly aware of the impact of early learning on the development of intellectual ability. The work of Benjamin Bloom at the University of Chicago suggests that half the variation in general school achievement can be predicted on the basis of characteristics that can be measured at the third grade level. The intellectual development theory of Piaget and the research done in the sixties stress the importance of the early years in a child's cognitive development. Burton L. White, director of the Pre-School Project of Harvard's Graduate School of Education, has recently completed an important book, *The First Three Years of Life* (Prentice-Hall, 1975), drawing on his extensive research in child development. Specific educational capabilities and tasks are identified for each phase of the child's physical and mental growth pattern. These guidelines can help parents and educators recognize and facilitate progress toward a child's greatest potential.

1. Leonard Breen, "Reading Instruction: Where Do You Fit In?" *School Media Quarterly* 3:129 (Winter 1975).

Ferne Johnson recently retired from the position of Consultant for Instructional Media, Fort Wayne Community Schools, Fort Wayne, Indiana, after a thirty-five year career in teaching and school librarianship. Jacqueline Morris is a media specialist at Leo High School, Grabill, Indiana, and an instructor in the Department of Library Science, Indiana University at Fort Wayne.

Emphasis on early childhood experience has been evident in federal funding, state plans, local involvement, and even neighborhood projects. There have been city-wide paid home helpers as well as numerous play centers staffed by volunteers to provide experiences with toys and with other children. Kindergartens have been established more extensively in public school systems. Some school districts have extended services downward to include the four-year-old. Illinois, for example, has mandated formal education for exceptional and handicapped three- and four-year-olds, and legislation has been proposed to permit the education of other preschoolers. Other states are following suit. Librarians interested in early childhood education are in great demand for children's services positions in both public and school libraries.

Libraries provide a natural setting for early childhood programs. Preschool story programs have been a part of the public library's children's services for almost as long as the agency has existed. Many school library media centers are currently equipped to serve kindergarten children, and with only slight changes in cognitive objectives could absorb the three- and four-year-olds.

Professionalism in materials selection is an area where librarians have a head start. They recognize excellence (and mediocrity) and are accustomed to deliberate analysis of media. Librarians responsible for preschool services have been able to acquire special training in child development by enrolling in appropriate classes, attending special institutes, participating in workshops, or engaging in some other form of continuing education. They are aware of child development stages from infancy through the early years of formal education, the effect of the child's environment on the rate of intellectual growth, the great need for positive experiences with media and with people in the development of language, and the important relationship between facility in language usage and the acquisition of reading skills. With this special training added to their knowledge of elements common to quality books, films, recordings, toys, and realia, children's librarians have the ability to plan and develop worthwhile media collections and innovative programs for young children.

In deciding which materials will enhance the learning processes, the early childhood media specialist knows that the visual, tactile, and auditory senses are particularly important. He or she recognizes that parents need to be *involved* in any early education program, since they can provide special insights into the child's needs and can establish an optimum home-learning environment. Adding ever-increasing knowledge of human development to a rich background of experience in preschool storytime and in promoting both the writing and the use of quality children's books, librarians are demonstrating their skill in structuring and executing effective program experiences for young children.

Library programs for preschoolers in the mid-seventies: *Where* are they? *What* are they? In what ways do they differ from those of earlier years? An

Opening More Doors

examination of library and educational literature provides some answers to
these questions; informal contacts at conferences, institutes, and workshops
add more information; and the correspondence files of library association preschool and early education committee chairpersons offer still another valuable
reference. As documentation of the value of early education continues, libraries of all sizes in all parts of the United States are expanding existing programs, developing new ones, and reaching out with appealing services.

One example of program expansion is the Lompoc, California, "Operation
PLENTY!"[2] This *P*ublic *L*ibrary *E*xtension *N*etwork for *T*iny *Y*oungsters
makes a variety of inexpensive, quality preschool books available to children
in many unusual non-library locations—automobile showrooms, veterinarians'
offices, Welcome Wagons, and furniture showrooms—as well as the more likely
places, such as Head Start centers, nursery schools, and mental health clinics.
In each book there is brief information for adults requesting that borrowed
books be returned to the public library. It is noted that the Welcome Wagon
has been the heaviest user of these books; thus, newcomers to the community
become acquainted with their public library very quickly.

Adding summer programs is one way school library media centers are expanding their services. In Dover, Pennsylvania, a school district with four elementary buildings selected the one having the largest seating capacity as the
site for their initial summer program.[3] Preschoolers were encouraged to borrow books, and a storytime was offered even though the library was open
only on alternate Tuesdays in July and August. Children could borrow as
many books as they wished; if the family were away when the two-week borrowing period ended, the books were due, without penalty, on the next library
day following the family's return.

In a summer media center program in Fort Knox, Kentucky, preschool
children were invited to borrow books, enjoy audio-visual media, and listen
to stories read by community volunteers.[4] An outgrowth of that project was
a weekly story reading/browsing session in each Fort Knox elementary school
for three- and four-year-olds. A beneficial spin-off was the evolvement of parent discussion groups.

Maryan Winsor, principal of a K–3 school in Wilmington, Ohio, believes in
getting to know each child as an individual.[5] Her unique method of accom-
plishing this goal is to visit each room for informal story reading—"The Principal's Story Time." Since the school is small, the visits are frequent and there
is time to share reactions to stories.

2. Paul F. Thompson, "Operation Plenty," *California Librarian* 36:9 (July 1975).
3. Louise Smith, "Library Facilities Easily Extended to Cover the Summer Vacation,"
School Media Quarterly 2:79 (Fall 1974).
4. Kyle McDowell and Thelma J. Estes, "Preschoolers Become Part of the Learning
Community," *Instructor* 85:124 (November 1975).
5. Maryan Winsor, "Mrs. Winsor's Story Time," *Instructor* 84:30 (February 1975).

In Fort Wayne, Indiana, another elementary school principal makes a different kind of contribution to the library program. He prepares cassette recordings of selected stories; these are added to the library media collection to be enjoyed by children individually or in groups.

In response to the directive to "develop a summer program to better prepare the kindergarten child for kindergarten," Loretta Farley, Head, Children's Services, Orange Public Library, Orange, California, created a "mini-school," complete with articulated goals and a structured two-hour program.[6] With twenty minutes in each block of time, the preschoolers were able to participate in imaginary journeys, enjoy free play periods, sit for storytime, interact with peers and adults for social development, experiment with crafts, and "explore their world" in a variety of other ways. Parents were involved in this program also. Sessions for parents were held both with the children and separate from them. Mothers learned about children's literature, how to use the library, and how to prepare their children for kindergarten.

In response to the emphasis on the parent's role as the child's first teacher, library programs geared to increasing the effectiveness of parent/child interaction continue to be developed and refined. As evaluation of these programs documents their value, children's librarians are coming to be recognized as effective educators of young children. Librarians can also help parents identify *their* role as "teacher," and increase their efficiency in that position.[7]

In an elementary school in Lafayette, Indiana, the school media specialist and parents cooperate in planning and administering a "Preschool Enrichment Hour," monthly from October through April.[8] A "story hour" for three- and four-year-olds includes—besides stories—films, puppet shows, finger-play activities and skits. Special school personnel—the librarian, counselor, speech therapist, kindergarten teacher, and others—acquaint parents with the school's total program. Toward the end of the program series the children's librarian describes the public library's summer fare for preschoolers and encourages parents to enroll their children.

The "Good Start" program began in the community room of a public housing project of sixty family units.[9] A federally funded project of the Elsmere Branch of the Glassboro (New Jersey) Public Library System, this program began with paperbacks and books borrowed from the state library. The

---

6. Loretta Farley, "Mini-Garten," *The Library Scene* 3:4–7 (September 1974).

7. Pauline Winnick, "Evaluation of Public Library Services to Children," *Library Trends* 22:370, 371 (January 1974); S. D. Wayland, "Measuring the Preschool Program," *Illinois Libraries* 57:24–26 (January 1975).

8. Frances A. Thompson, "A Pre-school Program in the Elementary School," *Hoosier School Libraries* 14:8–9 (December 1974).

9. Nadine J. Newcomb, "The Good Start Program: Reading Readiness in Action," *Library Journal* 99:541–45 (February 15, 1974); *School Library Journal* 20:31–35 (February 1974).

early success of this child/parent program justified its expansion to include two special sessions per week and brought increases in the materials collection and in space. In one of these two-hour segments the parents and children meet separately. The parent sessions include lectures, crafts activities, and experiences with books and audio-visual materials; children's sessions include directed activity, storytime, use of audio-visual materials, free play, and so on. In a second two-hour session parents and children meet together and assistance is given in meaningful parent-child interaction. The programs are planned in eight-week segments followed by eight optional weekly home visits. Use of the parent/child toy-lending program of the Far West Laboratory for Educational Research and Development has proved to be a valuable feature. An optional segment of the program is an information session on the Doman system of teaching reading to very young children. Periodic evaluation of the program consists of the completion of forms combined with parent interviews.

It has long been recognized that play is an important developmental activity for the preschooler.[10] However, the inclusion of this "child's work" in library programming and the necessary "tools" (toys) in the media collection constitute a relatively new but rapidly growing service in both public and school libraries. Word comes from libraries both large and small concerning the addition of toys and games to their collections. Some are used in connection with parent programs; some circulate much like books; others may be used in the library only. Since the toy-lending feature is not always associated with the preschool program exclusively, a number of the programs extend beyond that age level. As this phase of early childhood education develops, the line of demarcation between toys and realia becomes blurred. For the sake of simplicity we shall use the term toys to include all types of items used in children's play.

It would seem that many of the toy-related library programs either use or have been influenced by the recommendations of the Far West Laboratory for Educational Research and Development.[11] Although some of the programs which include toys have been noted earlier in this article, and others have been described in detail in other parts of this book,[12] the number of new and expanding programs seems to warrant additional citations.

An extensive program has developed in Connecticut under the leadership of Faith Hektoen, Connecticut State Library. In *Toys to Go: A Guide to the*

---

10. Association for Childhood Education International, *Play: Children's Business and a Guide to Play Materials,* 2d ed. (Washington, D.C.: A.C.E.I., 1974).

11. Far West Laboratory for Educational Research and Development, *A Guide to Securing and Installing the Parent/Child Toy-Lending Library* (Washington, D.C.: U.S. Govt. Printing Office, 1972).

12. See "Toys That Teach" by Nancy Orr and "Libraries and Parent Education" by Tommie Young.

Use of Realia in Public Libraries the evolvement of the state-wide program is described, the rationale expressed in detail, criteria for selection included, and much more.[13] Not only does this publication express the reasons for launching such a program and a description of how it was done, it also includes pertinent bibliographies, descriptions of procedures (including budgeting), and a statement on community reaction to the program. Appended is a list of public libraries in nearby states that have similar programs.

When interviewed by *School Library Journal,* Edythe O. Cawthorne, Coordinator of Children's Services, Prince George's County Memorial Library System, Maryland, discussed the toys and games program of their library system. She identified play as "the chief learning activity of preschool children" and "toys and games ... the first reading tools." She also pointed out that "...you don't develop readers by the use of books alone. There have to be motor skills, eye development and practice."[14]

Toy service began in the Mead Public Library, Sheboygan, Wisconsin, in June 1973.[15] Included in their rationale statement is the idea that children need a variety of toys to help them learn—including how to take care of things. Their goals? Fun, enjoyment, the enhancement of intellectual growth and development.

The Rent-a-Toy program in Irvington (elementary) School, Portland, Oregon, has a slightly different twist.[16] Students stock the library with games, puppets, cassettes, and other items. These are loaned for a period of one week to any child accompanied by a parent. With each item is an instruction sheet suggesting educational activities. The school's Parent Advisory Board has become interested in collecting discard articles such as jars, clothing, and fabric scraps to transform into toys.

One relatively small public library reports using live pets in connection with storytime. In describing the use of other realia in their preschool program, the children's librarian writes: "Leaves have been brought in to press and make prints ... flowers for May baskets. Porcupine quills fascinated the four- and five-year-olds, Indian items ... Japanese kimonos, fans, chopsticks.... Popping corn with the lid off the popper (onto a white sheet) was a great success...."[17]

Public and school libraries also offer a variety of outreach services to other agencies concerned with early childhood education. Children's librarians are

13. Connecticut Realia Committee, *Toys to Go: A Guide to the Use of Realia in Public Libraries* (Chicago: American Library Association, 1976).

14. Edythe O. Cawthorne, "Toys and Games—The First Reading Tools," *School Library Journal* 21:24–27 (April 1975).

15. "Toys for Loan: A New Library Service," *Library Journal* 99:1176 (15 April 1974) and *School Library Journal* 20:14 (April 1975).

16. Ibid.

17. Mrs. Victor Powell, unpublished letter, 4 March 1975.

frequent speakers for groups of nursery school teachers and day care personnel. They provide counsel, resource lists, demonstrations—a variety of services
to assist in the overall development of young children and to encourage the
effective use of books and other media. It is safe to assume that a children's
librarian is involved in some capacity in most preschool/parent education
projects.

The Kalamazoo (Michigan) Public Schools Division of Instructional Management, Elementary Department, has produced an attractive, useful "handbook of ideas for parents of preschool children," entitled *A Parent's Guide.*[18]
Prepared especially for parents in their Mother-Child Home Program, it stress-
es the importance of interacting with the young child in numerous home activities—playing, reading, talking, cooking, going on outings, and so forth. Included is a book list for both children and parents.

To teach parents how to help their children learn "to read well and with
enjoyment"[19] is the main objective of the course in the Jefferson County
School District, Madros, Oregon. Parents learn to select books for reading
aloud, to meet the needs of individual children, and to add to a child's personal library. While the course covers more than just preschool children, sharing literature with that group is stressed.

In a "Reading to Young Children" workshop, specific recommendations
are made to participants—parents, teachers, students.[20] These suggestions include ideas on book selection, *utilization of librarians* as competent resource
people, the attitude of the adult toward reading, techniques of successful
read-aloud experiences, and scheduling family reading time.

How can we be sure these programs are meeting the goals of their planners? In most cases some form of local evaluation has been used and some
formal studies have been made that include the preschool and parent programs. In an Illinois study, an evaluation was made of library storytelling
programs.[21] The conclusion was that the programs had a positive effect on
the children enrolled.

In describing a study done recently of "Exemplary Public Library Reading-
Related Programs for Children, Youth, and Adults," Pauline Winnick notes
some findings on preschool programs.[22] For instance, "Preschool programs
which provide activities for both preschool children and their mothers scored

18. *A Parent's Guide* (Kalamazoo, Michigan: Kalamazoo Public Schools, Division of
Instructional Management, Elementary Department, 1974).

19. Darrell Wright, "Children's Literature for Parents of Preschool Children," *School
Media Quarterly* 2:165–66 (Winter 1975).

20. Robert D. Lincoln, "Reading to Young Children," *Children Today* 3:28–30 (May
1974). Condensed in *Education Digest* 40:31–33 (October 1974).

21. Wayland, "Measuring the Preschool Program."

22. Winnick, "Evaluation of Public Library Services to Children."

higher on the effectiveness measure than programs limited to preschool children.... Measured effectiveness varied little according to the economic status of participants, or the current source of funding." Ms. Winnick goes on to say, "This study is a breakthrough, demonstrating that it is possible to measure the costs and the specific benefits derived by each child who is a participant in the library program, and to involve the parent as evaluator."

Among recommendations for future evaluations, Ms. Winnick recommends that "preschool children, 3 to 6 years of age, be given priority attention in user impact studies of community library services; that new media and new concepts of early childhood education be studied together with traditional activities for the youngest clientele."

A discussion of library services to preschool children and parents would be incomplete without some word on where librarians and other interested adults can look for help in increasing their knowledge and efficiency in this area. For the employed person with limited free time there are workshops and institutes. An examination of calendars (in library and educational journals) of events to come will identify this type of opportunity, stating dates, locations, and level of instruction.

Professional education organizations can identify their committees or divisions whose special interest is the preschool child. In the American Library Association the two committees responsible for this publication are dedicated to the welfare of that age group. In addition, bibliographies in this book and from other reliable sources represent much of the accumulated knowledge on early childhood education and child care and development. A good source of the most current thinking on the topic is, of course, current professional literature.

Through creative programming for *both* the "youngest clientele" and their parents, as well as assistance to other adults responsible for some phase of child development, librarians continue to increase the opportunities for children to participate in stimulating activities. Parents, nursery school teachers, social workers, day care personnel, and others interested in early childhood can be assured that librarians function as educators, information brokers, and program coordinators; and libraries can be expected to share the total responsibility that all locally funded institutions shoulder for strengthening and enhancing the opportunities for growth of the youngest citizens of the community.